A Theological Introduction
to the
Book of Psalms

A Theological Introduction to the Book of Psalms

The Psalms as Torah

J. CLINTON McCANN, Jr.

ABINGDON PRESS
Nashville

A THEOLOGICAL INTRODUCTION TO THE BOOK OF PSALMS:
THE PSALMS AS TORAH

This book is printed on recycled, acid-free paper.

Library of Congress Cataloging-in-Publication Data

McCann, J. Clinton, 1951-
 A theological introduction to the book of Psalms : the Psalms as Torah / J. Clinton McCann. Jr. : appendix by Nancy Rowland McCann.
  p. cm.
 Includes bibliographical references.
 ISBN 0-687-41468-7
 1. Bible. O.T. Psalms—Theology. I. McCann. Nancy Rowland.
 II. Title.
 BS1430 . 5 . M35 1993
 223 ' . 206—dc20   93-17475
                                                                                      CIP

Unless otherwise noted, all Scripture quotations are from the New Revised Standard Version Bible, Copyright 1989 by the Division of Christian Education of the National Council of the Churches of Christ in the USA. Used by Permission. All italics have been added by the author.

Those noted RSV are from the Revised Standard Version of the Bible, copyright 1946, 1952, 1971 by the Division of Christian Education of the National Council of Churches of Christ in the USA. Used by permission.

Excerpts from "Revelation" from *The Complete Stories* by Flannery O'Connor. Copyright © 1964, 1965 by the Estate of Mary Flannery O'Connor. Reprinted by permission of Farrar, Straus & Giroux, Inc.

Excerpts from *Interpreting the Psalms* by Patrick Miller. Copyright © 1986 by Fortress Press. Reprinted by permission of Augsburg Fortress.

Excerpts from "Expository Article on Psalm 13" by James L. Mays. First appeared in *Interpretation* 34, July 1980. Reprinted by permission of *Interpretation*.

Excerpts from "Prayer and Christology: Psalm 22 as Perspective on the Passion," James L. Mays. First appeared in *Theology Today* 42, October 1985. Reprinted by permission of *Theology Today*.

93 94 95 96 97 98 99 00 01 02 — 10 9 8 7 6 5 4 3 2 1

MANUFACTURED IN THE UNITED STATES OF AMERICA

In memory of my mother,

Nan Carter McCann,

and in honor of my father,

Jerry C. McCann, Sr.,

devoted students and teachers

of the Word

CONTENTS

PREFACE

My primary purpose in writing this book is to assist readers to hear the book of Psalms itself. Several preliminary suggestions and remarks may serve to facilitate that end:
1. Readers of this volume will need to have before them at all times an English translation of the Bible. This is especially important, since this volume does not provide a translation of the Psalms discussed. Frequent reference is made to the Psalms, of course, but also to numerous other passages of Scripture.
2. Unless otherwise noted, quotations from Scripture are from the New Revised Standard Version (NRSV). In citing the Psalms, I have used the English versification rather than the Hebrew.
3. I have not assumed that readers of this volume will know Hebrew; however, I do occasionally cite Hebrew words and phrases that are especially important. In each case, an English translation is provided.
4. Frequent reference is made to "the psalmist(s)." This is a traditional practice among interpreters, but the designation is problematic, since it may imply more individual creation of the Psalms than was actually the case. It should be remembered that we simply do not know who wrote the Psalms, where these authors or groups were located precisely, or when they wrote. To remind the reader of our lack of specific knowledge, I have not referred to a specific "psalmist."
5. My method of presentation of the theological content of the book of Psalms is primarily exegetical. Specific Psalms are interpreted in detail in order to arrive at theological conclusions. My primary interest is not how the Psalms functioned

in ancient Israel and Judah but rather how the Psalms address *us* in our time and place with a word from and about God, human life, and the life of the world.

6. In recent years, we have begun to realize more clearly that the interpreter herself or himself affects the interpretation of a text. I am no exception. My interpretation of the Psalms reflects who I am—namely, both a university-trained biblical scholar and an ordained pastor. While I write as a Christian theologian, I trust that my work will be of interest and benefit to persons with other convictions and commitments. I intend that this presentation will be accessible and useful (although in perhaps differing ways) to both specialists in biblical studies and to pastors, teachers, musicians, and others in the church.

The writing of any book is always a communal endeavor. There are many persons to whom I am indebted. The notes begin to indicate the persons from whom I have learned. I am grateful to the faculty and Board of Directors of Eden Theological Seminary, who granted me a sabbatical leave during the fall of 1990 to begin this project. I also received generous support in the form of a grant from the Association of Theological Schools in the United States and Canada (ATS). Participation in The Young Scholars Program, jointly sponsored by the ATS and the Pugh Charitable Trust, made available to me as a mentor Professor James L. Mays, whose wise counsel and friendship I deeply appreciate. My thanks to him and to the following persons who also read all or portions of the manuscript and from whose suggestions I have benefited: John Bracke, Steve Patterson, Beth Tanner, and Barbara Willock. Thanks are due also to Rex D. Matthews, Academic Books Senior Editor for Abingdon Press, for his interest in this project and his assistance in bringing it to completion; to Linda Allen of Abingdon Press for her careful copy editing; to Mary Swehla, Eden faculty secretary, for her many hours of labor with the manuscript; and to my wife, Nancy Rowland McCann, and daughters, Jennifer and Sarah, for their encouragement and support. Nancy Rowland McCann is responsible for the Appendix, which was developed with the valuable assistance of Hal H. Hopson.

Finally, I am grateful to many persons with whom I have taught and learned about the Psalms. These include students in the M.Div., D. Min., and Continuing Education programs at Eden Seminary as well as members of the following congregations or organizations in the St. Louis area (unless otherwise noted): Stanley White Presbyterian Church (Roanoke Rapids, N.C.); First Presbyterian Church of St. Louis; Hope Presbyterian Church; Bellefontaine United Methodist Church; Union United Methodist Church; St. Mark Presbyterian Church; Bonhomme Presbyterian Church; Kirkwood United Methodist Church; Webster Groves Presbyterian Church; Samuel United Church of Christ; Ladue Chapel Presbyterian Church; pastors of the Nebraska Conference, United Church of Christ; First Congregational United Church of Christ (Hastings, Neb.); Overland Presbyterian Church; Ferguson Presbyterian Church; Faith Presbyterian Church; Kirkwood United Church of Christ; Second Presbyterian Church; First Presbyterian Church, Kirkwood; Richmond Heights Presbyterian Church; Association of Presbyterian Christian Educators, Mid-Central Region; Trinity Presbyterian Church; St. Peter's United Church of Christ; pastors of the St. Louis Association, United Church of Christ; Holy Cross Lutheran Church; conferees at the Mo-Ranch Music and Worship Conference, 1992 (Hunt, Tex.); Glendale Presbyterian Church.

INTRODUCTION AND PURPOSE

The book of Psalms has been for centuries the primary resource for the liturgical and devotional life of the people of God. Its "varied and resplendent riches"[1] include magnificent hymns of praise, poignant outpourings of the soul in prayer, and earnest professions of the faithful. As Martin Luther put it in the sixteenth century:

> Where does one find finer words of joy than in the Psalms of praise and thanksgiving? There you look into the hearts of all saints, as into fair and pleasant gardens, yes, as into heaven itself. There you see what fine and pleasant flowers of the heart spring up from all sorts of fair and happy thoughts toward God, because of his blessings. On the other hand, where do you find deeper, more sorrowful, more pitiful words of sadness than in the Psalms of lamentation? There again you look into the hearts of all the saints, as into death, yes, as into hell itself. How gloomy and dark it is there, with all kinds of troubled forebodings about the wrath of God! So, too, when they speak of fear and hope, they use such words that no painter could so depict for you fear or hope, and no Cicero or other orator so portray them.
> And that they speak these words to God and with God, this, I repeat, is the best thing of all. This gives the words double earnestness and life. . . . Hence it is that the Psalter is the book of all saints; and everyone, in whatever situation he may be, finds in that situation Psalms and words that fit his case, that suit him as if they were put there just for his sake, so that he could not put it better himself, or find or wish for anything better.[2]

Because the book of Psalms has indeed been "the book of all saints," it is all the more strange and striking that the church in relatively recent years has virtually lost the Psalter. Not entirely, of course—every hymnal contains metrical versions of at least a few of the Psalms, and many hymnals include a selection of the Psalms that are designed for unison or responsive reading. Even so, the selection of Psalms seldom does justice to the rich variety of the Psalter. Hymnal editors prefer the upbeat Psalms of praise and thanksgiving, ignoring the Psalms of lamentation or complaint. The latter have disappeared almost completely from public worship.[3]

The church's loss has been intensified by the growing secularization of Western life and culture, which has been accompanied by an alarming growth of biblical illiteracy among people of faith. Early in the twentieth century, Rowland Prothero wrote a book entitled *The Psalms in Human Life and Experience*, in which he documents the widespread use and influence of the Psalms from the first century A.D. until 1900. His work amply demonstrates the truth of his opening statement: "So it is that, in every country, the language of the Psalms has become part of the daily life of nations, passing into their proverbs, mingling with their conversation, and used at every critical stage of existence."[4]

But such is the case no longer. The language of the Psalms is hardly part of our daily lives. If we ever hear it, we probably do not recognize it. And if we do recognize it, it probably sounds to us strange and archaic. The "book of all saints" has become a lost treasure.

Fortunately, amid all the evidence that the Psalter has been lost, there are encouraging signs of an effort to recover the Psalms. Biblical scholars are making the Psalter the focus of intensive research and discussion, and they are advancing new perspectives on the Psalms. Pastors and teachers are beginning to rediscover the Psalter as an invaluable resource for their own spiritual lives and for the spiritual development of their congregations. *The Revised Common Lectionary* suggests a lesson from the Psalter for each Sunday, and at least some congregations are hearing a wide selection of the Psalms on a regular basis. Composers are writing new and compelling musical settings for the Psalms, and the singing of the Psalms is becoming more frequent in public worship. The new *United Methodist Hymnal*, for instance, includes a "Psalter." It contains the texts of one hundred Psalms as well as a musical refrain for each psalm, so that the Psalms can be either read or sung. The new *Presbyterian Hymnal* also contains an entire section of Psalms, and the Presbyterian Church (U.S.A.) is currently producing a Psalter for use by congregations. The use of the Psalms is also experiencing a renewal among Episcopalians, Lutherans, and Roman Catholics. In short, an attempt is being made to recover the book of Psalms. (See the appendix for further details and a list and description of resources.) Perhaps it is not too much to hope that the language of the book of Psalms may again become "part of the daily life of nations," that the Psalter may again become what it has been for generations of God's people—"the book of all saints."

It is the purpose of this book to contribute to the church's recovery of the book of Psalms. For those who read this book, it is my hope that it will assist you in making the book of Psalms *your* book. I hope it will enable you to make its praises *your* praises and its prayers *your* prayers. And finally, I hope that the teaching contained in this book will help to prepare you to be instructed by the book of Psalms itself.

This final hope serves to describe the particular emphasis of this volume—the Psalms as *torah*, "instruction." It is clearly important to recognize that the Psalms have been and should continue to be used as human words to God—as hymns and prayers. As the appendix suggests, the Psalms are meant to be sung; and as Eugene H. Peterson puts it, "The Psalms are prayer" and thus "Tools for Prayer."[5] But it is also important to recognize that the Psalms have been preserved and transmitted by the faithful as *God's word to humans*. As Klaus Seybold recognizes on the basis of the Psalter in its final form, the Psalter has more the character of a catechism than a hymnbook or prayerbook:

> the existing Psalter now takes on the character of a documentation of divine revelation, to be used in a way analogous to the *Torah*, the first part of the canon, and becomes an *instruction*

manual for the theological study of the divine order of salvation, and for meditation.[6]

Thus the Psalms are not just human words *to* God. They are also words *about* God. They teach us about God; they reveal who God is. Because the Psalms are instructive and revelatory, it is appropriate that the Psalms were received and transmitted ultimately as Scripture—as a word *from* God to humanity.

In a sense, this understanding of the book of Psalms is very old (see below), but it has been largely forgotten in the twentieth century. My attempt to contribute to its recovery is motivated by the fact that recent biblical scholarship has provided a solid, scholarly foundation for understanding the Psalms as "instruction."[7]

RENEWING AN OLD APPROACH

To understand fully the rationale and significance of approaching the Psalms as *torah*, it will be helpful to review briefly the interpretation of the book of Psalms in the twentieth century. At the beginning of this century, the Psalms were understood primarily as the work of pious individuals who composed prayers and songs either for their private devotional use or in response to a particular historical event. Thus scholars were intent upon determining and attempting to describe the authors of the Psalms, to discern the historical circumstances of their composition, and to date each psalm as specifically as possible. The tendency was to date most Psalms very late (third to second century B.C.) and to view them as evidence of an individualized spirituality that was superior to the corporate worship of earlier centuries of Israelite and Judean history.

Early in the twentieth century, German scholar Hermann Gunkel became convinced of the inadequacy of this approach. He noted the many references in the Psalter to liturgical activities (singing, dancing, shouting, sacrifice, prayer, etc.) and places (temple, house of the Lord, gates, courts, etc.), and he concluded that the Psalms were as much or more related to the corporate worship of ancient Israel than to the meditation of pious individuals. Gunkel's approach is known as form criticism; he classified the Psalms into various forms or types or genres, and then sought to determine where each type would have fit in the worship life of ancient Israel.[8] Actually, Gunkel was not willing to break completely with the earlier approach to the Psalms. He still maintained that the Psalms were composed late in Israelite history by individuals, but he also claimed that the authors based their poetic creations upon prototypes that had originated in the worship life of an earlier period.

Sigmund Mowinckel is credited with taking the next logical step. According to him, the Psalms are not spiritualized copies of earlier prototypes. Rather, they represent the actual songs and prayers that were produced for and used in the public worship of Israel and especially of Judah before the destruction of the Jerusalem Temple in 587 B.C. Mowinckel's approach is known as the cult functional method. In practice, form criticism and the cult functional method are inseparable. The goal is first to categorize by form and then to determine a setting in which a particular psalm may have functioned in the life of ancient Israel or Judah.[9]

Form criticism and the cult functional method have been the dominant approaches to interpreting the Psalms in this century, and they are still alive and well. To be sure, the methods have developed over time. The categories for classifying the Psalms have been refined and extended, and many new life-settings for the Psalms have been proposed.[10] Even as many scholars continue to practice and refine form criticism and the cult functional method, however, other scholars have been pointing out the limitations of these approaches and have been calling for new directions.

One of the clearest of these calls was issued in 1968 by James Muilenburg, whose presidential address to the Society of Biblical Literature was entitled "Form Criticism and Beyond."[11] Muilenburg did not desire to abandon form criticism entirely, but he did suggest that this dominant method be supplemented by an approach that he called rhetorical criticism.

According to Muilenburg, scholars should take seriously the rhetorical or literary features of each psalm in order to discern "the actuality of the particular text."[12] In other words, while form criticism is interested in what is typical or generic about a psalm in order to categorize it, rhetorical criticism is interested in what is unique about a psalm in order to appreciate its individual character. Muilenburg's call did not go unheeded. Rhetorical criticism has joined form criticism as a major interpretative approach to the book of Psalms.

While Muilenburg suggested only that form criticism be supplemented, other scholars have been harsher in their criticism of the method. In 1976, Brevard Childs observed that form criticism "seems now to be offering diminishing returns."[13] Childs suggested that the move beyond form criticism be made by directing attention to the final form of the Psalter in order to determine how the meaning of individual Psalms may be affected by their titles and by their placement in the canonical form of the Psalter. In the past fifteen years, scholars have devoted a great deal of attention to investigating the shape of the Psalter. The most extensive investigation has been by Gerald H. Wilson, who has demonstrated conclusively that the Psalter is not simply a random collection of songs and prayers.[14] Wilson, Childs, and others have noted that Psalm 1 forms an introduction to the Psalter, the effect of which is to inform the reader that the Psalter is not merely a collection of liturgical resources but is to be read and heard as a source of *torah*, "instruction" (the Hebrew word occurs twice in Ps. 1:2; see chap. 1).[15] As Childs suggests, songs and prayers that originated as the response of faithful persons to God have been appropriated and presented as God's word to the faithful.[16]

The implications of this approach were highlighted in 1986 by James L. Mays, whose presidential address to the Society of Biblical Literature was entitled "The Place of the Torah-Psalms in the Psalter."[17] Like Childs, Mays pointed to the introductory claim of Psalm 1, but he also emphasized the fact that torah-Psalms are interspersed throughout the Psalter. The effect is to orient the faithful to hear the Psalms as God's instruction. In terms of interpretative approaches to the Psalms, the effect of the canonical shape of the Psalter is this: "Form-critical and cult-functional questions are subordinated and questions of *content and theology* become more important."[18] Childs makes a similar point:

> I would argue that the need for taking seriously the canonical form of the Psalter would greatly aid in making use of the Psalms in the life of the Christian Church. Such a move would not disregard the historical dimensions of the Psalter, but would attempt to profit from the shaping which the final redactors gave the older material in order to transform traditional poetry into Sacred Scripture for the later generations of the faithful.[19]

The treatment of the Psalms in this book takes seriously the importance of the final form of the Psalter. Part I deals with the shape of the Psalter; and based upon the shape of the Psalter, the organizing principle for Parts II–IV is "instruction." To be sure, the results of form criticism have not been ignored. For instance, Part II deals with what form critics identify as hymns or songs of praise; Part III deals with what form critics identify as prayers of lament or complaint; and Part IV deals primarily with what form critics identify as Psalms of assurance/trust and songs of Zion. In each case, however, the question of form and setting is subordinate to questions of content and theology. Similarly, the results of rhetorical criticism have not been ignored. Frequently, I shall point out the importance of a psalm's structure and call attention to the significance of repetition, which N. H. Ridderbos suggests is the most important rhetorical device in the Psalter.[20] In each case, however, my interest is not simply in literary matters as such, but rather in how structure creates or reinforces theological meaning and how repetition highlights theological content. In short, I am interested in what the Psalms teach—about God and God's rule, about humanity and its role, about sin and forgiveness, about vengeance and compassion, about salvation and the life of the faithful. I have organized this theological content under the headings of Instruction for Praise and Praise as Instruction

(Part II), Instruction for Prayer and Prayer as Instruction (Part III), and Instruction for Profession and Profession as Instruction (Part IV). Because the Psalms figure prominently in the New Testament, the concluding chapter considers the use of the Psalms as testimony to Jesus Christ.

As suggested above, to approach the Psalms as instruction is not new. So-called pre-critical interpreters (that is, biblical interpreters before the rise of historical criticism in the late eighteenth and nineteenth centuries) regularly gave attention to the question of how the Psalms instruct the faithful; it would never have occurred to them *not* to ask questions of content and theology. For instance, in "The Author's Preface" to his *Commentary on the Book of Psalms,* John Calvin recognized that the Psalter serves "to *teach* us the true method of praying aright"; that "there is no other book in which we are more perfectly *taught* in the right manner of praising God;" and that "although the Psalms are replete with all the precepts which serve to frame our life to every part of holiness, piety, and righteousness, yet they will principally *teach* and train us to bear the cross."[21] In short, Calvin approached the Psalms as instruction for prayer, praise, and the life of faith. His categories are similar to those of Parts II–IV of this volume. In a sense, my approach is quite old.

What *is* new in this book is that the recovery of an old approach to the Psalms is based on the research and conclusions of contemporary biblical scholars such as Childs, Wilson, and Mays, who are taking seriously the shape of the book of Psalms. In doing so, they are not being "pre-critical"; they are not adopting the methods of an earlier era. After all, what could be more *historically* honest and *critically* appropriate than to approach the book of Psalms the way its shapers intended—as *torah,* "instruction"? The canonical form of the Psalter reminds us that the Psalms were not preserved to serve as a source for reconstructing the liturgical history of ancient Israel and Judah, although they may be used in such a task (as form critics do). Neither were the Psalms treasured as examples of beautiful poetry, although they are (as rhetorical critics recognize). Rather, the Psalms have been preserved and treasured because they have served to instruct the people of God about God, about themselves and the world, and about the life of faith.

One final word: Instruction is not something that takes place primarily in a classroom. The people of God have been instructed by the Psalms as they have read and meditated upon them in private devotion; and above all, they have been instructed as they have read and heard and sung the Psalms in public worship. Liturgy inevitably is instructional. Liturgy shapes minds and hearts; it moves and transforms; it creates a new vision of reality.[22] Because this is the case, and because most persons will encounter the Psalms in worship, this book concludes with an appendix entitled "The Singing of the Psalms." It discusses the use of the Psalms in worship, especially the singing of the Psalms; and it also lists and describes resources for singing the Psalms.

PART I:

THE SHAPE OF THE BOOK OF PSALMS

CHAPTER 1

THE PSALMS AS TORAH, THEN AND NOW

Biblical scholars have traditionally struggled with the question of where to begin an exposition of the book of Psalms. There are so many psalms to choose from—150. And there are several different types. Should one begin with the songs of praise? Should one begin with the prayers of lament or complaint? Should one begin with the psalms of thanksgiving, or perhaps the entrance liturgies, or the psalms that recite Israel's saving history? Seldom has it occurred to scholars to begin at the beginning. In fact, Psalm 1 has often been relegated to *last* place in treatments of the Psalms. Psalm 1, along with Psalms 19 and 119, is a torah-psalm, a psalm in which the concept of *torah*, "instruction" (NRSV "law"; see below) is preeminent (see Pss. 1:2; 2; 19:7; 119:1, 18, 29, 34, 44, plus twenty more times in Ps. 119). The effect of treating Psalms 1, 19, and 119 last has been to relegate the concept of *torah* to one of minor significance in understanding the Psalms.[1] But having made the decision to take seriously the canonical shape of the Psalter, we shall begin at the beginning—Psalm 1. The effect is to elevate the concept of *torah* to one of central significance in understanding the Psalms. As suggested above and again in this chapter, the Psalms are to be heard as God's instruction to the faithful.

This chapter begins and ends with an interpretation of Psalm 1; the middle consists of a briefer look at the other torah-psalms, Psalms 19 and 119. Chapter 2 will begin with an interpretation of Psalm 2, which is linked to Psalm 1 and also forms part of the introduction to the Psalter.

PSALM 1:1-2

Upon reading the first two verses of the Psalter, one is struck immediately by two things. First, there is a sharp contrast drawn between the wicked/sinner/scoffer and people whose "delight is in the law of the LORD" (v. 2). Verses 3-6 will sharpen this contrast even further, eventually identifying the latter type of people as "the righteous" (vv. 5-6). We shall return below to the significance of this contrast.

A second observation is the focus on "law" at the very beginning of the Psalter. For many biblical scholars and non-specialists alike, this emphasis on "law" has proven problematic. One interpreter captures well the nature of the problem: "It's not difficult to see why someone might find Psalm 1 a quite insufferable Psalm about a quite insufferable fellow. There he sits, day and night, brooding and fretting over the law. What a pedant!"[2] For Christian readers of Psalm 1, "the righteous" may sound even worse than pedants. Christian readers are inclined to hear Psalm 1 in the light of New Testament affirmations such as "we hold that a person is justified by faith apart from works prescribed by the law" (Rom. 3:28; see Gal. 2:16). When this is the case, then "the righteous" of Psalm 1 begin to sound like the kind of people who were frequently Jesus' opponents and whom Jesus accused of *self*-righteousness (see Matt. 25:27-28; Mark 2:15-17; Luke 18:9-14). The inclination is to be rather suspicious of people whose "delight is in the law of the LORD." If Psalm 1 is an introduction to the Psalter, then the Psalter does not sound too promising or inviting.

To hear Psalm 1:1-2 this way, however, is to misunderstand it entirely (as well as to misunderstand the New Testament, in which Paul can say in Rom. 3:31 that "we uphold the law," and in which Jesus says in Matt. 5:17, "Think not that I have come to abolish the law and the prophets; I have not come to abolish them but to fulfill them"). The problem stems from translating the Hebrew word *torah* as "law." The Hebrew word can mean "law" in the sense of specific injunction (Exod. 12:49) or a collection of legislation (Exod. 24:12; Deut. 4:8); however, it essentially means "instruction."[3] The introductory verses of the Psalter have an entirely different sound when *torah* is so translated:

> Happy is the one who does not walk
> in the counsel of the wicked,
> and in the way of sinners does not stand,
> and in the seat of scoffers does not sit;
> but rather who delights
> in the instruction of the Lord,
> and upon God's instruction meditates day and night.
> (my translation)

The introduction to the Psalter is anything but an invitation to pedantry, legalism, or self-righteousness. On the contrary, it is an invitation to be *open to God's instruction* and to the reality of *God's* reign in the world (see chap. 2).

We shall return below to the question of how openness to God's instruction means that one is "happy," but for now it is important to point out that *the Torah* for Judaism is the five books of Moses, Genesis through Deuteronomy (which include not just "laws" in the strict sense but also stories). It is highly significant that the Psalter also consists of five books (Psalms 1–41, 42–72, 43–89, 90–106, 107–150).[4] The editors of the Psalter wanted readers to grasp the analogy between *the Torah*, God's "instruction" *par excellence*, and the Psalter. In short, the Psalter is to be read and heard as God's instruction to the faithful. Regardless of the fact that the Psalms originated as the response of faithful persons to God, they are now to be understood also as God's word to the faithful.

Obviously, the concept of *torah* was both very significant and very positive for the shapers of the Psalter. To appreciate this more fully, we turn now to Psalms 19 and 119 before returning to Psalm 1.

PSALM 19

The difficulty interpreters have had with the torah-psalms is indicated by the fact that many scholars divide Psalm 19 into two separate psalms. Psalm 19A (vv. 1-6) deals with creation, and Psalm 19B (vv. 7-14) deals with *torah*. Supposedly, there is no relationship between the two.[5] To bisect Psalm 19, however, is to fail to appreciate a carefully constructed poem and to miss entirely its message about the *torah* of the Lord.

Granted, verses 1-6 talk about creation. Without literally being able to speak, the heavens offer powerful and convincing testimony to the glory of God. No corner of the universe is unreached by this witness (note the three occurrences of "end" in vv. 4 and 6). When verses 7-13 are heard immediately following verses 1-6, the message about God's *torah* is clear. The "instruction of the Lord" (v. 7; my translation) is built into the very structure of the universe. It is as fundamental and reliable and close-at-hand as the progression of day and night (v. 2), the rising and setting of the sun (v. 6). And the impact of *torah* is just as far-reaching as the circuit of the sun—to the end of the heavens.[6]

A different translation of verse 7 helps to reinforce the connection between verses 1-6 and verses 7-14. A traditional translation is as follows:

The law of the LORD is perfect,
reviving the soul; (RSV, NRSV)

"Perfect" is a misleading translation, because we almost inevitably hear connotations of moral perfection. The Hebrew word means "sound," "complete," "all-encompassing." While "soul" is an acceptable translation, the Hebrew word can also mean "life," "living being" (see Gen. 2:7). The following translation sounds quite different from the traditional:

The instruction of the Lord is all-encompassing,
restoring human life; (my translation)

Psalm 19:1-6 has described the all-encompassing circuit of the sun; similarly, verse 7 proclaims that God's instruction is all-encompassing. As God is responsible for creating the heavens, the sun, and the progression of day and night, so the *torah* of God is responsible for constantly re-creating human life (the Hebrew participal suggests that the activity of "restoring" is continual). To discern the unity between 19:1-6 and 19:7 is to begin to appreciate the psalmist's daring claim and the psalms' radical implications. The psalmist's claim about *torah* means that we live not by our own cleverness, initiative, achievement, or possessions (see 19:10), but rather as Jesus said, we live "by every word that comes from the mouth of God" (Matt. 4:4; see Deut. 8:3).

For the psalmist, to be open to God's instruction is the only way to live. That is why *torah* is to be so desired (19:10) and why in keeping *torah* "there is great reward" (19:11). Like verse 7, verses 11-13 can be misleading. The mention of "great reward" and being "warned" (v. 11) and "blameless" and "innocent" (v. 13) may lead us to conclude that keeping *torah* is simply a matter of being rewarded for obeying a set of rules. But the matter is more complex; moral perfection or moral blamelessness is not what the psalmist has in mind. I prefer to hear verse 11 and the conclusion of verse 13 as follows:

> Moreover by them is your servant *instructed*;
>   there is great consequence in keeping them. . . .
> Then I shall be *whole*,
>   and *acquitted* of great transgression. (my translation)

Verses 12 and 13 suggest that the psalmist, despite the best of intentions, will inevitably sin. The good news is that, despite inevitable errors and hidden faults, life is possible—a life of wholeness and integrity (v. 13; the Hebrew word usually translated "blameless" is from the same root as the word in v. 7, which is usually translated as "perfect"), a life in which great consequences are possible (v. 11). This "abundant life" (John 10:11) is not the result of human achievement; its source is God, and it depends on God's forgiveness (19:13, "acquitted of great transgression"). Similarly, Jesus' admonition to "be

perfect" in Matthew 5:48 is not an affirmation of human potential but rather an acknowledgment of God's rule and the reality of the forgiveness of sins. To "be perfect" or "blameless" or
"whole" is not to be sinless, but rather to be open to the torah
of the Lord on which human life constantly depends. Such is
the bold claim of Psalm 19, a claim to which we must return
below as we explore the meaning of the terms *happy* and
righteous in Psalm 1.

The movement of Psalm 19 is completed by the final verse.
Verses 1-6 had God and the whole cosmos in view; verses 7-13
narrowed the focus to God's instruction and humanity; and
verse 14 focuses even more narrowly on the individual human
life:

> Let the words of *my* mouth and
> the meditation of *my* heart
>   be acceptable to you,
>   O LORD, my rock and my redeemer.
> (emphasis added)

The "words" of verse 14 repeats the Hebrew word translated
as "speech" in verses 2-3. In short, this final verse is the
psalmist's prayer that his or her life be in tune with the music
of the spheres, the very structure of the universe. Having
heard verses 1-13, we know that the psalmist's audacious
request is not impossible with God. The psalmist's words will
be acceptable to God as he or she opens the self to the all-encompassing, life-giving instruction of the Lord. It would be
difficult to imagine a more powerful and eloquent affirmation
of the significance of God's *torah*, unless perhaps it is Psalm
119.

PSALM 119

As with Psalm 19, it is easy to illustrate with Psalm 119 the
difficulty scholars have had with the torah-psalms. Consider
the following opinion of the Psalm: "Tedious repetitions, poor

thought-sequence, apparent lack of inspiration reflect the arti-
ficiality of the composition."[7]

Actually, the composition is more artistic than artificial. The
psalm consists of twenty-two stanzas, one for each letter of the
Hebrew alphabet. Each line within a particular stanza begins
with the same letter. Every stanza except one (vv. 9-16) contains at least one occurrence of the word *torah*, and every line
of the poem contains either the word *torah* (25 occurrences) or
a synonym for *torah*. The structure of Psalm 119 reinforces the
theological content. In short, *torah* is pervasive and all-encompassing. It applies to everything from *A* to *Z* (or in Hebrew,
from *ālep* to *tāw*).

As Westermann has recognized, "If a person succeeds in
reading this psalm's 176 verses one after the other at one
sitting, the effect is *overwhelming*."[8] Precisely! And that is exactly the effect the psalmist intended. For the psalmist, the
importance of *torah* is overwhelming! Apart from God's instruction, there is nothing worthy to be called life.

It is not surprising that Psalm 119 shares much of the vocabulary of Psalms 1 and 19 (see, for instance, vv. 1, 15-16, 23-24, 72,
98, 103, 127, 133). An examination of the opening line of Psalm
119 must suffice:

> Happy are those whose way is blameless,
>   who walk in the instruction of the Lord.
> (my translation)

In fact, every word of Psalm 119:1 occurs in either Psalms 1 or
19. It is clear from verse 176 that the blamelessness involved is
not moral perfection, for the psalmist confesses: "I have gone
astray like a lost sheep" (literally, "perishing sheep"; *perish* is   אבד
the same word used to describe the way of the wicked in the
last verse of Psalm 1!). Likewise, the psalmist's being "happy"
must involve something very different from automatically
reaping the benefits of following a set of rules. Somehow, the
psalmist's "happiness" cannot be incompatible with the persecution and scorn she or he experiences (vv. 22-23, 42, 51, 61, 69,
84-87, 95, 110, 121, 134, 141, 150, 157, 161) and with sorrow and
affliction (vv. 28, 50, 71, 75, 92, 107, 153). Psalm 119 poses

sharply the question: What does the psalmist mean by
"happy"? Obviously, it has everything to do with orienting
one's life to being instructed by God. But what does the
"happy" life look like in practice? We shall address this question when we return to Psalm 1.

It is interesting to consider the possibility that an earlier
form of the Psalter may have consisted of Psalms 1–119.[9] If
so, this would mean that at one stage of its existence the
Psalter itself was encompassed by what Psalms 1 and 119
affirm is all-encompassing—the instruction of the Lord. It
would be yet another instance of how literary structure
reinforces content and theology. But even if Psalm 119 was
never the conclusion of the Psalter, its current position in
the Psalter is still important. As Wilson suggests, it is a
central and dominating presence in the fifth and final book
of the Psalter; and it is intended to instruct the faithful in
how to live in reliance on the Lord.[10] When taken in relation
to Psalms 1 and 19, as well as portions of other psalms that
emphasize the centrality of *torah*, the effect is as follows:
"Taken together, this harvest of texts contains a profile of an
understanding of the Lord's way with people and the world
that is organized around torah. Torah applies to everything."[11]

This is precisely the claim Psalm 1 makes as it introduces
the Psalter: Torah applies to everything!

PSALM 1:3-6

Psalm 1 makes this bold claim by developing the contrast
that it introduces in the first two verses of the Psalter. If
torah applies to everything, it applies especially to the way
human life is lived and to the way life turns out (note the
repetition of "way" in vv. 1 and 6). As Psalm 19 puts it, there
is "great consequence" (v. 11; my translation) in being instructed by God. The contrast between "the righteous" and
"the wicked" is developed carefully, comprehensively, and
artistically.

The structure, movement, vocabulary, and imagery of the psalm combine to emphasize that there should be absolutely no confusion about the two ways and their results. For instance, the adversative particles at the beginning of verse 2 and in the middle of verse 4 serve to draw the contrast as sharply as possible ("but"; Hebrew *kî 'im*). The negative particle at the beginning of verse 4 is emphatic, "Not so!" (Hebrew *lō'-kēn*). The word *therefore* at the beginning of verse 5 makes the whole psalm sound like a sort of mathematical proof—clear, logical, straightforward. In short, there can be no doubt about it: those who are instructed by God are "happy," and the wicked are "not so."

The effect of the structure and movement of the psalm is reinforced by the vocabulary. The very first word of the psalm is *happy*, and the very last word is *perish*. Such are the results of being open or of failing to be open to God's instruction; the way one chooses makes the difference between life and death. The contrasting choices are highlighted a final time in verses 5-6 by the repetition of *way* (v. 6), *righteous* (vv. 5, 6), and *wicked* (vv. 5, 6). The pattern of the repetition is important too: "wicked . . . righteous . . . righteous . . . wicked." This *abba* pattern (chiasm) is frequent in Hebrew poetry, and its effect is to call attention to the middle element(s). In this case, "the righteous" are preeminent, both literarily and theologically. While "the wicked" perish on the periphery of verses 5-6, "the righteous" are the very center of God's attention. One must choose between the center and the periphery, between life and death; there is no other ground.

My mention of "ground" turns our attention to the central image or metaphor of Psalm 1, which we find at the literary center of the psalm (v. 3). The righteous "are like trees planted by streams of water." In short, the righteous have a place to be grounded, to take root, to be nourished, and to grow. One aspect of this metaphor involves fruitfulness. The righteous "yield their fruit in its season, . . . In all that they do, they prosper." In contrast, there is nothing fruitful about the wicked. They "are like chaff" (v. 4), the waste product that is discarded after the fruitful wheat has been harvested. Thus we see how the central metaphor of Psalm 1 reinforces the effect of structure, movement, and repetition. There are two sharply contrasting ways. The righteous are happy, fruitful, prosperous, alive. The wicked are "not so," and their way "will perish."

Having heard the message of Psalm 1 and seen it reinforced in several ways, we are probably less likely to think of its author as a pedant than we are to dismiss him or her as a naive optimist, the original positive thinker. How can anyone suggest that the righteous will always be "happy" and always "prosper"? What about the so-called "real world," where might makes right and the fittest survive and crime usually does pay? These kinds of questions make it imperative that we now turn to the question we have previously postponed: What does the psalmist mean by "happy"? Similarly, what does it mean to "prosper"? Obviously these two questions cannot be answered apart from others: Who are "the righteous" and "the wicked"? And what does it mean to be instructed by God?

To begin to answer these complex questions, it is helpful to notice that another aspect of the central metaphor of Psalm 1 has to do with movement.[12] The wicked are not only unfruitful, but they are also driven away by the wind (v. 4) and "will not stand" (v. 5). They have no foundation. The righteous, on the other hand, are well-grounded; it is their solid foundation that enables them to be nourished and grow (see Jer. 17:7-8, which points out the importance of rootedness for prosperity and fruitfulness). This aspect of the metaphor gives us such a helpful clue as to what the psalmist means by "happy."

It must also be noted from the outset that the psalmist was no naive optimist any more than he or she was a self-righteous, simple-minded legalist. The psalmist knew about the "real world." The psalmist knew that the wicked appear to do very well for themselves. The psalmist knew that obedience to a set of rules does not guarantee that one will be healthy or rich or famous or popular. The psalmist knew that the righteous suffer. All one has to do is read the rest of the Psalter:

do not fret over those who *prosper* in their *way* [note the vocabulary from Psalm 1],

over those who carry out evil devices. (Ps. 37:7)
For I was envious of the arrogant;

I saw the prosperity [*shalom*] of the wicked (Ps 73:3).

In fact, prayers of complaint are the dominant type in the Psalter; and a regular feature of these prayers is the presence of powerful and prominent enemies (the wicked, the foes, the evil-doers, etc.) who persecute the righteous psalmist (see as early in the Psalter as Ps. 3:1-2). If the wicked can experience such prosperity or peace, then the prosperity of the righteous must consist of a peace, which, as Jesus put it, is "not as the world gives" (John 14:27).

Taking a clue from the central metaphor of Psalm 1, to be "happy" or to "prosper" is to have a solid foundation, to have a place to stand (vv. 1, 5). For the psalmist, that foundation is to delight in and to meditate upon *torah*, to be constantly open to God's instruction. Taking such a stand or such a stance enables one to live with purpose and integrity in a world of confusion (see Pss. 19:13; 119:1 where "integrity" would be a more auspicious translation than "blameless"). It enables one to live with hope in a world full of despair, and it enables one to perceive the mystery of life where others may perceive only the misery of life.

A remarkable illustration of what Psalm 1 means by "happy" or "righteous" is the story of Natan Sharansky. A Soviet Jew, Sharansky was jailed in 1977 for speaking out in favor of the right to emigrate from the Soviet Union, advocating free speech, and refusing to cooperate with Soviet authorities. He was subjected to a horrible ordeal, including periods of solitary confinement and near starvation. When he was finally released in 1986, the one possession he carried to freedom was a copy of the book of Psalms in Hebrew. Shortly before his release, Soviet guards had confiscated the book, returning it only after Sharansky lay down in the snow and refused to take another step. The book had been a gift from his wife, Avital.

Her constant efforts to win her husband's release, along with the book of Psalms she had given him, turned out to be Sharansky's source of strength during his imprisonment. In a review of Sharansky's autobiography, *Fear No Evil* (the title of which alludes to Ps. 23:4), Patricia Blake writes:

> Sharansky's spiritual resources were even more remarkable. For comfort and guidance he memorized the Psalms in Hebrew and chanted them often. . . . Like another mathematician before him, Archimedes, he reckoned that *with a place to stand on* he could move the earth. And so he did.[13]

Sharansky's story has nothing to do with naive optimism or self-righteous legalism. It has everything to do with delighting in and meditating on *torah*; it has everything to do with being open to God's instruction; it has everything to do with being open to God's presence in the face of unimaginable opposition and open to God's power to transform the most hopeless of situations. In short, it has everything to do with having a "place to stand." For Sharansky, the book of Psalms functioned precisely as its editors intended—both to open the faithful to God's guidance and instruction and to serve as a source of that instruction. In short, the Psalms enabled Sharansky to maintain what he refers to as his " 'spiritual independence against the kingdom of lies.' "[14] Actually, his "spiritual independence" could be more aptly described as his absolute *dependence* on God. To open persons to such dependence on God as they face the wicked ("the kingdom of lies") is the purpose of Psalm 1 as an introduction to the Psalter. This dependence upon God, this openness to God's instruction, is what Psalm 1 means by "happy" and "prosper." As Sharansky discovered and demonstrated to the world, openness to God's instruction has "great consequence" (Ps. 19:11).[15]

For the Christian, it is helpful to think of openness to God's instruction in terms of what Paul calls "maturity." It is revealing that Paul's description of maturity is strikingly similar to the central metaphor of Psalm 1. Paul's metaphor is a human body rather than a tree, but for Paul, maturity involves both fruitfulness/growth (compare Ps. 1:3) and a grounding that prevents being driven as if by the wind (compare Ps. 1:4). His description is as follows:

> The gifts he [Christ] gave were that some would be apostles, some prophets, some evangelists, some pastors and teachers, to equip the saints for the work of ministry, for building up the body of Christ, until all of us come to the unity of the faith and of the knowledge of the Son of God, to maturity, to the measure of the full stature of Christ. We must no longer be children, tossed to and fro and blown about by every wind of doctrine, by people's trickery, by their craftiness in deceitful scheming. But speaking the truth in love, we must grow up in every way unto him who is the head, unto Christ, from whom the whole body, joined and knit together by every ligament with which it is equipped, as each part is working properly, promotes the body's growth in building itself up in love. (Eph. 4:11-16)

What Psalm 1 means by delighting in and meditating on *torah* is analogous to what Paul means by reaching "the measure of the full stature of Christ." Becoming like Christ can never be a simple matter of obeying a set of rules, because we simply do not know what Christ would do or say in all the contemporary circumstances we face. "Speaking the truth in love" may be a helpful guide, but it does not give specific directions or prescriptions. And obviously, becoming like Christ can never be a matter of *self*-fulfillment or *self*-righteousness. For the Christian, it is not a matter of Christ replacing the Psalms. Rather, both the Psalms and Christ call persons to depend on God. In a way that is analogous to Psalm 1, becoming like Christ means to depend on God at all times, to be dedicated and open to God's guidance and instruction. For Paul, such a stand or such a stance means that one can grow, even into "the measure of the full stature of Christ."

Homiletician Tom Long tells a true story about his father, which can help us to picture a contemporary instance of meditating on *torah*, of becoming like Christ.

In the 1960s, the elder Mr. Long was appointed by the president of Erskine College in Due West, South Carolina, to head a committee to study the implications of new federal civil rights legislation. The provisions of the law required schools to sign documents stating they were in compliance with the legislation in order to receive federal funds for grants and loans. In preparation for his task, Long did not consult lawyers or labor over legal briefs or study the details of the legislation. Instead, he read the Bible and the confessions of the church, day after day, week after week. When the committee made its report, the recommendation was remarkable and surprised many people: that Erskine College without delay comply fully with the civil rights legislation, not as a means to keep federal funds, but as a matter of faithfulness to God and as a witness to Jesus Christ.[16] What Long had done was to meditate on *torah*, opening himself to God's instruction. No simple-minded legalism was involved; there were no rules to be followed. Nor was any self-righteousness involved; if anything, Long was putting himself and the college in a difficult position. In a time of national and institutional crisis and uncertainty, Long found "a place to stand" and the strength to stand there. He demonstrated what it means to be open to God's instruction, to be growing into "the measure of the full stature of Christ." In terms of Psalm 1, he showed what it means to be "happy," to "prosper," to be among "the righteous." As Mays suggests about the "way of the righteous," "The fulfillment is not so much a reward as a result of life's connection with the source of life."[17]

By describing "the righteous" as those who are open to God's instruction and who live in dependence on God, we have anticipated the content of chapter 2 and its discussion of the reign of God; and we have also put ourselves in a position to describe "the wicked." The wicked are those who see no need to be open to God's instruction or to live in dependence upon God. In short, the wicked are those who consider themselves autonomous, which literally means "a law unto oneself." The wicked are self-instructed, self-directed, self-ruled. If the fulfillment of the way of the righteous "is not so much a reward as a result of life's connection with the source of life," then the fulfillment of the way of the wicked is not so much a punishment as a result of cutting oneself off from the source of life. In short, wickedness contains the seeds of its own destruction, as suggested by Gary Chamberlain's translation of Psalm 1:6*b*, "but an evil life leads only to ruin."[18]

In her short story "A Good Man Is Hard to Find," Flannery O'Connor offers a penetrating portrayal of what the Psalms call "the way of the wicked." A character called the Misfit, an escaped convict, has come upon a minor automobile accident. The grandmother of the family recognizes him, so he decides he must kill the whole family before stealing their clothing and their car. The grandmother tries to talk him out of it. She asks him to pray and allow Jesus to help him. "I don't want no hep," the Misfit answers. "I'm doing all right by myself."

For Psalm 1 and the rest of the Psalter, wickedness is essentially the conviction that we are doing all right by ourselves. It is a matter of whom we trust, on whom we depend. The story continues.

> "Jesus was the only One that ever raised the dead. . . . And he shouldn't have done it. He thrown everything off balance. If He did what He said, then it's nothing for you to do but throw away everything and follow Him, and if He didn't, then it's nothing for you to do but enjoy the few minutes you got left the best way you can—by killing somebody or burning down his house or doing some meanness to him. No pleasure but meanness."

The Misfit shoots the old woman, and one of his buddies, Bobby Lee, returns from having killed the rest of the family. Bobby Lee is excited and shouts "Some fun!" The Misfit scolds him, saying, "It's no real pleasure in life."[19]

The Misfit is right. In the absence of faith—failing to trust God or to believe what Jesus said he did—we are left to ourselves to do whatever we can or will. One thing is as good as another. What may seem like pleasure is an illusion; it's simply selfishness, or worse, meanness. Failing to be open to God's instruction, failing to live toward becoming like Jesus, there is no way to be what Psalm 1 calls "happy," no way to "prosper." In short, "it's no real pleasure in life."

The psalmist's understanding of the righteous and the wicked may well be alarming to those of us who live in a culture where perhaps the highest virtue is autonomy. We live in what Walker Percy has called "the Century of the Self."[20] We are taught to be self-reliant, self-made. Our goal is to be self-fulfilled, self-actualized. Wanting or needing help is interpreted as a sign of weakness; and we view it as a sign of emotional health and maturity when a person can say, "I'm doing all right by myself." While the psalmist's perspective may be disturbing to us, it certainly explains a lot about ourselves. It helps us to understand why one of the most highly developed, healthiest, wealthiest, and most intellectually sophisticated societies in the history of the world consistently fails to produce people who are "happy." The condition of the church and the culture in the late twentieth century reinforces the need to recover the book of Psalms for what it can teach us. Richard Osmer has recently called for Protestant churches to "recover an authentic sense of the piety of their own heritage." He characterizes this piety in a phrase borrowed from John Calvin: "a teachable spirit."[21] In a real sense, "a teachable spirit" is what Psalm 1 means by being "happy" and "righteous"—open to God's instruction and to growth toward the full measure of the stature of Christ.

As an introduction to the Psalter, Psalm 1 announces that the *torah* of the Lord, God's instruction, applies to everything! It is an invitation to be open to God's instruction and to use the content of the rest of the Psalter as one source of God's instruction. We turn now to that content, beginning with Psalm 2, the message of which underlies everything else the Psalms will teach us.

CHAPTER 2

THE PSALMS AND THE REIGN OF GOD

As scholars have begun to take seriously the shape of the Psalter, they have realized that Psalms 1 and 2 together form an introduction to the Psalms. While Psalm 1 informs the reader that the whole collection is to be approached and appropriated as instruction, Psalm 2 introduces the essential content of that instruction—the Lord reigns! Nothing about God, the world, humanity, or the life of faith will be properly learned and understood apart from this basic affirmation.

PSALM 2

The literary links between Psalms 1 and 2 are a major clue that the two psalms are meant to be read as a literary unit. The most obvious link is the repetition of "blessed" or "happy" at the beginning of Psalm 1 and the end of Psalm 2. This *inclusio* or envelope-structure is a frequent device in the Psalms. It is the poet's way of literarily holding things together. To "take refuge in" God (2:12) is precisely what Psalm 1 means by "the way of the righteous"—that is, openness to God's instruction and living in dependence upon God alone.

There are several other impressive literary links between Psalms 1 and 2. For instance, the NRSV's "plot" in 2:1 is the same Hebrew word that is translated "meditate" in 1:2. Meditation on God's instruction is effectively contrasted with

thinking that is empty or purposeless. Such thinking characterizes "the wicked," and it leads to destruction. Not surprisingly, the destiny of the enemies of the Lord and the Lord's
anointed is described in Psalm 2 in the same terms that are
used in Psalm 1: "you will *perish* in the *way*" (2:12, compare
1:6).[1] In short, Psalm 2 portrays in corporate terms ("nations,"
"peoples," "kings," "rulers"—vv. 1-2, 10) what Psalm 1 described in terms of the individual—that is, the contrast between the righteous, who are open to God's instruction and
God's rule, and the wicked, who plot among themselves and
oppose God's reign.

The recent history of interpretation of Psalm 2 has really not
focused attention on the reign of God, but rather on the theology of the Davidic monarchy. Form critics categorize Psalm 2
as a royal psalm. Actually, this category is characterized not
by a particular form or structure, but by *content*. All the psalms
that deal with the Judean or Israelite king or the monarchy are
included among the royal psalms (see also Pss. 18, 20, 21, 45,
72, 89, 110, 144).[2] Psalm 2 has been traditionally understood as
part of the ceremony for the coronation of a Davidic king.
Historically speaking, this approach to Psalm 2 is quite plausible. It is easy to picture a priest or prophet speaking on God's
behalf to the king (the Lord's "anointed"; v. 2) as he prepares
to take office:

> "I have set my king on Zion, my holy hill." (2:6)

To which the king responds:

> I will tell of the decree of the LORD:
> He said to me, "You are my son;
> today I have begotten you." (2:7)

This plausible historical reconstruction fails, however, to
deal with the final form of Psalm 2 as a literary product and its
placement within the Psalter. It thus fails to appreciate that
Psalm 2 is really more about the reign of God than about the
Davidic monarchy. Notice, for instance, that when Psalm 2
addresses the kings and rulers, the admonition to them is as

follows: "Serve the LORD with fear" (v. 11). The real issue in Psalm 2 is this: Who rules the world? Is it the kings and rulers of the nations and peoples (vv. 1-2)? Or is it the Lord (vv. 10-12)? For Psalm 2, the answer is clear: The Lord reigns! The choice of an anointed one (v. 2, Hebrew "messiah"), a son (v. 7) is not unimportant; however, it is simply one means by which the Lord exercises sovereignty. As Mays suggests, "the inaugural of the anointed is a declaration that 'the Lord reigns' in the midst of a history whose powers deny it."[3]

PSALM 2, THE ROYAL PSALMS, AND THE ENTHRONEMENT PSALMS

Gerald Wilson provides further evidence for the claim that Psalm 2 should be heard primarily as an affirmation of God's sovereignty rather than the sovereignty of the Davidic monarchy. He points out that three royal psalms occur at crucial points in the Psalter, and he takes this fact as an important clue to the editorial purpose of the Psalter. Psalm 2 occurs very near the beginning of Book I (Psalms 1–41); Psalm 72 concludes Book II; and Psalm 89 concludes Book III. Both Psalms 2 and 72 speak favorably of the Davidic monarchy, but when Book I and II are read in conjunction with Book III and its concluding Psalm 89, "a new perspective is achieved."[4] The first thirty-seven verses of Psalm 89 speak favorably of the Davidic monarchy, but verses 38-51 recount the rejection of the Davidic monarchy and the failure of the covenant. Wilson describes the effect of the final form of Books I–III as follows:

At the conclusion of the third book, immediately preceding the break observed separating the earlier [i.e. Books I–III] and later books [i.e., IV–V; Psalms 90-106, 107–150], the impression left is one of a covenant remembered, but a covenant *failed*. The Davidic covenant introduced in Ps 2 has come to nothing and the combination of three books concludes with the anguished cry of the Davidic descendants [see 89:46]. . . . It is to this problem of the failure of YHWH to honor the Davidic covenant that Ps 89 directs its plea. How long? And it is with this plea that the first part of the Psalter ends.[5]

As Wilson further suggests, Books IV–V of the Psalter are intended "as the 'answer' to the problem posed in Ps 89." In particular, Book IV is the "editorial 'center' of the final form of the Hebrew Psalter."[6] And the primary affirmation or "answer" that Book IV makes is this: The Lord reigns! The dominant collection in Book IV is composed of Psalms 93, 95–99, the enthronement psalms,[7] all of which explicitly affirm that the Lord is king or that the Lord reigns (93:1; 95:3; 96:10; 97:1; 98:6; 99:1). It is the enthronement psalms "which become the theological 'heart' of the expanded final Psalter."[8] In short, the central theological affirmation of the Psalter is this: The Lord reigns!

For Wilson, this conclusion has an important historical dimension; that is, the final form of the Psalter addressed the theological crisis of exile (loss of temple, loss of land, loss of monarchy) by affirming God's sovereignty. In addition, and more relevant for our purposes, Wilson's conclusion is further testimony to the significance of Psalm 2 and its meaning in the context of the final form of the Psalter. Given the crucial placement of the enthronement psalms at the editorial "center" of the Psalter, we can say even more emphatically that Psalm 2 is more about God's reign than about the existence of the Davidic monarchy. It introduces the essential content that the Psalter intends to teach—the Lord reigns!

To be sure, Psalm 2 and the whole Psalter recognize that the reign of God exists amid continuing opposition—from the nations and peoples (2:1), the kings and rulers of the earth (2:2), the wicked (Psalm 1). That is to say, Psalm 2 as part of the introduction to the Psalter, as well as the other royal psalms and the enthronement psalms, serves to give the Psalter in its final form an eschatological orientation. It is probable that Psalm 2 and the other royal psalms functioned in pre-exilic Judah as liturgies for royal coronations or other ceremonies. It is even possible that the enthronement psalms were used at some Temple festival to celebrate or re-enact the enthronement of the Lord. But in the final form of the Psalter, the royal psalms and enthronement psalms function differently; they function eschatologically. As Mays suggests: "They no longer refer only to what happened in the cult, but as well as to what was promised in prophecy. Psalm 2, reread as a vision of the goal of history, puts the torah piety of Psalm 1 in an eschatological context."[9]

The eschatological orientation of the final form of the Psalter—the affirmation that God's rule is effective *now* and will ultimately be fully manifest—means that the reader is called to a decision.[10] Who is sovereign? In whom or in what will one trust? Will one trust the apparent power of the kings and rulers of the earth, the wicked? Or will one trust the Lord? Psalm 1 and Psalm 2 together suggest that the righteous are those who are open to God's instruction and God's rule, who "take refuge" in God. The righteous are those who, amid competing powers and claims, decide to trust God, to wait upon the Lord. The nature of this decision is further evident from the content and context of the enthronement psalms.

PSALM 96

Form critics classify the enthronement psalms as a sub-category of the hymns or songs of praise. As we shall see in chapter 3, the hymns consist typically of an invitation to praise God (96:1-3) and the reasons for praising God (96:4-5). A unique feature of Psalm 96 is that it extends the invitation to praise by using the language of another enthronement psalm, Psalm 29 (96:7-9; see Ps. 29:1-2). Psalm 96, however, addresses the invitation to "families of the peoples" rather than to "heavenly beings" (29:1). In short, Psalm 96 makes it clear that the Lord's sovereignty is to be effective on earth as well as in heaven. The crucial proclamation occurs in 96:10: "The LORD reigns!" (RSV). Verses 10-13 then proceed to describe the effects of God's reign, the most prominent of which is the establishment of justice or the setting of things right on earth (the verb *špṭ* in 96:10, 13 does mean "to judge," but the purpose or positive effect of judgment is justice; the noun form of the root is *mišpāṭ*, "judgment" or "justice," and occurs in 97:2, 8; 99:4).

What is revealing, however, is that justice has not yet been established. The Lord "is coming to judge" and "will judge"

(v. 13). The proclamation of God's reign is made before all the evidence is in; it is eschatological. In fact, the evidence would suggest that God does *not* reign! Here again, we must take seriously the final form of the Psalter. As Wilson points out, Psalms 93–99, which are at the editorial heart of the Psalter, respond to a covenant that appears to have failed—exile, destruction, the loss of the land and the monarchy. Not surprisingly, Psalm 96 and the other enthronement psalms have their closest scriptural parallels in the material of Deutero-Isaiah (Isaiah 40–55), which also represents a response to the exile and the appearance that the Lord did *not* reign. To a defeated and discouraged people, the prophet proclaims good tidings (Isa. 40:9; 41:27; 52:7; the same Hebrew root *bśr* is translated "tell" in Ps. 96:2). Despite appearances, the Lord is doing a "new thing" (Isa. 42:9; 43:19; 48:6) to which the proper response is a "new song" (Isa. 42:10; see also Ps. 96:1). The prophet's good news involves God's reign (Isa. 52:7; see also Ps. 96:10), to which folk respond by singing for joy (Heb. *rnn*; Isa. 52:8 as well as 42:11; 44:23; 49:13; 54:1; see also Ps. 96:12). Justice is the Lord's purpose (Isa. 42:1, 3-4; see also Ps. 96:10, 13), and God's purpose includes the nations and peoples (Isa. 42:1; 45:22-23; 49:1-6; 52:10; 55:4-5; see also Ps. 96:7, 10, 13). Deutero-Isaiah also joins Psalm 96 in emphasizing that "the gods of the peoples are idols" (Ps. 96:5; see Isa. 40:19; 41:21-29; 44:9-20; 46:1-7).

In both Psalm 96 and Isaiah 40–55, the proclamation of God's reign occurs in a context (literary, historical, or both) in which it appears that God does *not* reign. In short, a decision must be made. Can we, shall we "sing to the Lord a new song" amid the same old daily realities? Can we, shall we say "the Lord reigns" when the forces of evil seem overpowering? Can we, shall we say "the world is firmly established" when things around us seem to be falling apart? Can we, shall we wait for the Lord and the establishment of God's justice? For the psalmist, the answer is clear: We can, we shall, we must. The only possible source of happiness is to proclaim God's reign and to "take refuge in" God (Ps. 2:12). A decision is crucial, as Psalm 95 also emphatically suggests.

PSALM 95

Psalm 95 begins like a typical hymn with the invitation to praise (vv. 1-2, 6) and reasons for praise (vv. 3-5, 7*ab*). But verses 7*c*-11 are not typical, leading scholars to find other labels for the psalm—"liturgy of divine judgment" or "prophetic exhortation." More important than form, however, is the effect of verses 7*c*-11. They call the reader to a decision in response to the proclamation of the reign of God (v. 3). This effect is achieved in several ways. For instance, the language and imagery of Psalm 95 recall the exodus event and the subsequent response of the people. The mention of "sea" in verse 5 is reminiscent of Exodus 15:1, and "dry land" in verse 5 recalls the path the people took through the sea (Exod. 14:16, 22, 29; 15:19). In this context, "my work" in verse 9 is certainly an allusion to the exodus. The exodus event culminated in a song that concluded with the affirmation "The LORD will *reign* forever and ever" (15:18). This sequence of deliverance and proclamation of God's reign should have led to obedience; but almost immediately the people complained about their deliverance, first at Marah (Exod. 15:22-27) and again shortly at Massah and Meribah (Exod. 17:1-7; Ps. 95:8). The question the people raise at Massah and Meribah is essentially the question of whether God really reigns: "Is the LORD among us or not?" (Exod. 17:7). The question calls for a decision.

The call to decision is even more explicit in Psalm 95:7*c*: "O that today you would listen to his voice!" The three-part poetic line of verse 7 has the effect of isolating and thus emphasizing verse 7*c*. Verse 7*c* is transitional; it culminates the hymnic affirmations of verses 1-7*b* and also introduces the issue of verses 8-11. In the book of Exodus, the sequence of deliverance and proclamation of God's reign should have led to immediate obedience, but instead it led to immediate complaining. Psalm 95 says, in effect, "Do not repeat that mistake." In your place and time—your *today* (v. 7*c*)—listen to God's voice. In response to the proclamation of the reign of God (vv. 1-7, esp. v. 3), obey (the Hebrew root *šm'*, translated "listen" in v. 7*c* is often translated "obey") instead of complaining. In short, Psalm 95 calls for a decision in response to the reign of God.[11]

There is a rabbinic tale that culminates in a reference to Psalm 95:7c and emphasizes the significance of its call to decision. Rabbi Yoshua ben Levi finds the prophet Elijah, and he asks him when the Messiah will come. Elijah tells the rabbi that he can find the Messiah at the city gates among the poor. The rabbi goes and initiates the following exchange:

> "Peace unto you, my master and teacher."
> The Messiah answered, "Peace unto you, son of Levi."
> He asked, "When is the master coming?"
> "Today," he answered.
> Rabbi Yoshua returned to Elijah, who asked, "What did he tell you?"
> "He indeed has deceived me, for he said, 'Today I am coming' and he has not come."
> Elijah said, "This is what he told you: 'Today if you would listen to His voice.' " (Psalm 95:7).[12]

The reign of God, represented in the tale by the coming of the Messiah, is experienced as a decision made *today*. It is eschatological—effective *now* but also to be awaited.

PSALMS 1 AND 2 AND THE SHAPE OF THE PSALTER

As a paired introduction to the Psalter, Psalms 1 and 2 tell us how to approach the whole book. The Psalms call persons to live under the reign of God, to "take refuge in" God. And the Psalms are instruction for those who make this decision. As Mays suggests about Psalms 1 and 2: "This intricate pairing as introduction says that all psalms dealing with the living of life under the Lord must be understood and recited in light of the reign of the Lord and that all psalms concerned with the kingship of the Lord are to be understood and recited with the torah in mind."[13]

The book of Psalms suggests that those who choose to live under the reign of God will praise God, pray to God, profess their faith in God. Thus the Psalter is instruction for and by praise (Part II), prayer (Part III), and profession (Part IV). The concluding chapter of this volume will move beyond the Psalms themselves to the life of Jesus and the New Testament. This move is quite logical (or at least, *theo*logical) in the light of Psalm 2, the other royal psalms, and the enthronement psalms we have discussed in this chapter. The Psalms proclaim God's reign and invite persons to live under God's rule. So did Jesus (see Mark 1:14-15). The Psalms offer instruction for what it means to trust God and live under God's reign. So did Jesus, one of whose primary titles was "teacher." In other words, both the instruction of the Psalter and the teaching of Jesus are eschatological. Both call the hearer to decide *now* to live under God's rule and to *await* the consummation of God's rule. This relationship between the teaching of the Psalms and the teaching of Jesus is captured movingly by Flannery O'Connor in a story, the title of which is based on the KJV of Psalm 2:1: "Why Do the Heathen Rage?" In the story, a dominating mother laments the fact that her grown son will not take over the responsibilities of running the family farm when her husband has an incapacitating stroke. Instead of attending to practical matters, the son "read books that had nothing to do with anything that mattered now." One day the mother picked up one of the books and was struck by a passage her son had underlined. It was from a letter of St. Jerome to Heliodorus, who had abandoned his avowed calling:

> "Listen! The battle trumpet blares from heaven and see how our General marches fully armed, coming amid the clouds to conquer the whole world. Out of the mouth of our King emerges a double-edged sword that cuts down everything in the way. Arising finally from your nap, do you come to the battlefield! Abandon the shade and seek the sun."

The final lines of the story record the mother's reaction: "This was the kind of thing he read—something that made no sense for now. Then it came to her, with an unpleasant little jolt, that the General with the sword in his mouth, marching to do violence, was Jesus."[14]

Both the Psalms (Psalm 2 and the entire collection) and the Gospel announce the jolting claim that God rules the world now and will ultimately consummate that rule. Both the Psalms and the Gospel call for a decision that often seems, amid the practical matters of the so-called real world, to make "no sense for now." As we shall see more fully in the conclusion to this volume, it is not coincidental that the Gospel writers drew heavily upon the Psalms in order to comprehend and describe the life, death, and resurrection of Jesus, who proclaimed and embodied the reign of God in a way that seemed to most of his contemporaries to make "no sense for now."

PART II:

INSTRUCTION FOR PRAISE AND PRAISE AS INSTRUCTION

CHAPTER **3**

PRAISE AND IDENTITY: THE MAJESTY OF GOD AND THE GLORY OF MORTALS

The Hebrew title of the book of Psalms is *tĕhillîm*, "Praises." Although the hymns or songs of praise are outnumbered in the Psalter by the prayers of lament or complaint, the title "Praises" is appropriate. Even the prayers of lament or complaint move toward praise (see Pss. 13:5-6; 22:22-31; etc.).[1] So does the Psalter as a whole. Whereas prayers of lament or complaint dominate Books I–III, hymns or songs of praise are dominant in Books IV–V.[2] Thus praise becomes the goal of the Psalter in the same way that praise is the goal of human life. Praise is fundamental. As Westermann puts it:

> The praise of God in Israel never became a cultic happening, separated from the rest of existence, in a separate realm, that had become independent of the history of the people and of the individual. Rather, it occupied a central place in the total life of the individual and the people before God. . . . The praise of God occupied for Israel actually the place where "faith in God" stands for us. In Israel it was a fundamental of existence that God was and that therefore they believed in him. . . . On this still unshaken basis the clearest expression of the relationship to God was the act of praising God.[3]

In short, praise is the offering of the whole self to God. To be sure, it involves what happens in worship; but more than that, praise involves essentially who we are and what we do at every moment. It is, as Westermann again suggests, a "mode of existence":

> There is no real, full existence that does not in some way honor, admire, look up to something. . . .
> If the praise of God, as the Psalms express it, belongs to existence, then the directing of this praise to a man, an idea, or an institution must disturb and finally destroy life itself. The Psalms say that only where God is praised is there life.[4]

The Psalms make a radical claim: To praise God is to live, and to live is to praise God! Thus praise has everything to do with God's identity and activity as well as with human identity and activity. "Rejoice in the LORD, O you *righteous!*/Praise befits *the upright*," says Psalm 33:1 (emphasis added). In other words, instruction for praise builds upon the foundation of Psalms 1 and 2. Praise is the "mode of existence" characterized by openness to God's instruction (Psalm 1) and the acknowledgment of God's reign (Psalm 2). Praise is fundamental.

A final word of introduction is necessary before turning to the Psalms themselves. Patrick D. Miller, Jr., writing about praise in the psalms, concludes: "One cannot fully comprehend what took place and takes place in praise without feeling the emotions of exultation and delight, shouting and dancing."[5] What may have the power to produce feelings of exultation and delight is the singing of the Psalms, an experience I strongly recommend (see the appendix). Undoubtedly, many of the psalms, especially the hymns or songs of praise, were meant to be sung and were accompanied by shouting and dancing. The response Duke Ellington's version of Psalm 150 elicited from its hearers arrives at the essence of praise. Jazz historian Stanley Dance describes it as follows: "In Barcelona, in the ancient Church of Santa Maria del Mar, the enthusiasm was such that the congregation burst into the aisles to participate in the finale, 'Praise God and Dance' [Psalm 150]. The music and the message of the concert seemed to transcend language barriers without difficulty."[6] Such is the nature of praise. Praise of God is a "mode of existence" that thrusts us toward the universal, toward the transcendence of "barriers without difficulty."

One of the most memorable photographs of recent decades appeared on February 12, 1990. It depicted "Archbishop Desmond Tutu dancing for joy at his home in the black township of Soweto after hearing that Nelson Mandela would be released from prison."[7] Tutu is also either singing or shouting, and beside him an unnamed woman, hands upraised, is laughing exuberantly. What about us? What, if anything, makes us laugh, sing, dance, shout for joy? This question is awesomely important in the late twentieth century, when the common "mode of existence" among us is often either boredom or disappointment. Walker Percy is right: "As John Cheever said, the main emotion of the adult Northeastern American who has had all the advantages of wealth, education, and culture is disappointment." Percy continues by pointing out that work, family life, school, and politics are disappointing; then he turns to the church: "The churches are disappointing, even for most believers. If Christ brings us new life, it is all the more remarkable that the church, the bearer of this good news, should be among the most dispirited institutions of the age."[8]

If Percy is even approximately correct, then it is all the more important that we be instructed by the Psalms. They reveal to us a "mode of existence" that is desperately lacking among us. The Psalms tell us both who God is and what God does, and thus who we are and what we are to do. To listen and to learn is to walk the way that leads to life. The result is not disappointment, but rather what Psalm 1 means by "happy." We shall proceed exegetically by examining four hymns as we seek to hear what the Psalms teach us about God, ourselves, and the world.

PSALMS 117 AND 150

In the space of two short verses, Psalm 117 manages to convey essentially what praise is all about. The typical structure of a hymn is evident: Verse 1 is the summons to praise

God, and verse 2 gives the reasons for praising God. What is particularly noteworthy is that the invitation is extended to "all you nations" and "all you peoples," not just to Israel or to Judah or to some group of the faithful. Praise inevitably pushes toward universality, toward the transcendence of barriers. It is the "mode of existence" God desires for *everybody!* The claim is simple but breath-taking: Praising God is the goal of human life! But the Psalter is not content with even that sweeping claim. The Psalter concludes with a crescendo of praise, and the last note is this (Ps. 150:6):

> Let everything that breathes praise the LORD!
> Praise the LORD!

In short, praising God is the goal of every living thing, the goal of all creation! The Hebrew for "everything that breathes" is *kōl hannĕšāmâ* (literally, "all the breath"). The word *breath* recalls the Genesis traditions: the creation of humanity (Gen. 2:7) and the flood story in which the proper goal of human and animal life was not realized (see Gen. 7:22). Against this background of destiny gone awry, Psalm 150 teaches us that the proper mode of existence for humankind and all creation is relatedness to God. In short, to live authentically is to praise God, and to praise God is to live.

While Psalm 150 is reminiscent of the early chapters of Genesis, Psalm 117 recalls the book of Exodus. The reasons for praising God in verse 2 are God's "steadfast love" (*ḥesed*) and "faithfulness" (*ĕmet*). These two words form the climax of God's self-revelation to Moses in Exodus 34:6. It is not sufficient on the basis of Exodus 3:14 to say simply that God's identity is mysterious, although mystery is involved. Nor is it sufficient on the basis of Exodus 1–15 to say simply that God acts on behalf of the poor, although God indeed does. Rather, we must conclude finally that God's identity is inextricably bound to God's choice to be related to a sinful humanity. After an initial affirmation of God's sovereignty (Exod. 15:1-18), the people's response to the deliverance at the sea is to gripe and complain (Exod. 15:22–17:7). After their initial affirmation that "we will be obedient" (Exod. 24:7; see also 24:3), the people's response to the covenant at Sinai is to break immediately the first two commandments. After Exodus 24:3, 7, the very next time the people speak is to request Aaron "to make gods for us, who shall go before us" (32:1). Only after the people have revealed their inevitable sinfulness does God finally identify God's self as:

> "The LORD, the LORD,
> a God merciful and gracious,
> slow to anger,
> and abounding in *steadfast love*
>   and *faithfulness*." (Exod. 34:6, emphasis added)

By recalling God's self-revelation in Exodus 34, Psalm 117 grounds the reasons for praising God in God's fundamental identity. God's "loyal love" and "faithfulness" will ultimately allow God to do nothing other than love the world and its sinful inhabitants.[9] The good news that the Psalms teach us is that human life is incomprehensible apart from God's love for the world, for "all nations" and "all peoples" (see John 3:16-17). To praise God is to understand that one's fundamental mode of existence is relatedness to God. For the psalmists, relatedness to God is the only source of human identity that can possibly avoid disappointment and destruction. In short, to praise God is the only possible way to be "happy"; indeed, it is the only possible way to experience what Scripture calls "life." The same essential instruction can be heard in a very different song of praise, Psalm 8.

PSALM 8

Scholars unanimously classify Psalm 8 as a hymn or song of praise, even though it does not conform at all to the typical structure we saw in Psalm 117. Nevertheless, the structure of Psalm 8 provides important clues about the content and theology of the psalm. The most obvious literary feature of the psalm is the refrain (vv. 1, 9). The structural boundaries of the psalm focus clearly on the Lord and the Lord's sovereignty: "How majestic is your name in all the earth!"

While the boundaries of the psalm focus on God, the structural center of the psalm focuses directly on humanity (v. 4):

> what are human beings that you
> are mindful of them,
> mortals that you care for them?

To understand how the psalm works compositionally it is important to note that the same Hebrew word underlies "how" in verses 1 and 9 and "what" in verse 4, so that the eye and mind of the reader are drawn to the boundaries and the center of the psalm. As Brueggemann suggests, the structure of Psalm 8 is a clue to the crucial interpretative issue; that is, how are the boundaries and the center of the psalm to be held together?[10] In short, how are the "glory and honor" of humanity (v. 5) to be understood in relation to the "majesty" and "glory" of God (vv. 1, 9)?

This crucial interpretative issue is a question of identity. Who is God? What is humanity? Another literary clue as to how the psalmist intends us to answer these questions is provided by the repetition (vv. 1, 6, 7, 9) of the little word *all*.[11] The "allness" of God's majesty is given by God to humanity (vv. 6-7, esp. "you have put *all* things under their feet"). The repetition of "all" in verses 6-7 affects how we hear the refrain when it recurs in verse 9. Verse 9 is an exact verbal repetition of verse 1, but the sense now is different precisely because the psalmist has told us that the majesty of God in "all the earth" includes the glory and dominion of humanity. The identity of God and the identity of humanity are inseparable. The boundaries of the psalm must be held together with the center.

But how? Again, the structure enables us to move toward an understanding of content and toward theological conclusions. Both structurally and theologically humankind is at the very center of things (v. 4). The seemingly small and insignificant human creature (v. 3) has been given "glory and honor" (v. 5) and "dominion" over "all things" (v. 6). To fail to take seriously the centrality of humanity in the created order is to risk ignoring our God-given responsibility to exercise dominion, to be faithful stewards of "all things." But the structure of the psalm also suggests that human glory and dominion are *derivative*. Structurally and theologically human dominion is bounded, delimited by God's sovereign majesty. To focus on the boundaries of Psalm 8 without an awareness of the center is escapist; human beings do have a central role in the created order. The greater danger, however, is that we focus on the center without an awareness of the boundaries. To put human dominion at the center of things without the context of God's sovereignty is positively dangerous. When the exercise of human dominion ceases to be derivative, when it becomes unbounded, then dominion is in danger of becoming disaster. The possible consequences are becoming frighteningly evident—the depletion of the ozone layer, the "greenhouse effect," the threat of nuclear annihilation, the problem of hazardous waste, the disappearance of plant and animal species. At a recent conference at the Missouri Botanical Garden in St. Louis, David Brower, a former executive of the Sierra Club, stated well the danger of ignoring the boundaries of human dominion: "For 250 years, we've learned how to take the Earth apart—we're very good at it. But we've learned very little about putting it back together."[12]

What Psalm 8 teaches us is that it is simply not sufficient to "take the Earth apart." If the centrality of human dominion does not contribute to the majesty of God "in all the earth," then God-given dominion has been replaced by human autonomy. The result is death and destruction—for the earth, for ourselves, for future generations.

It is not naive to say that the first step in addressing the environmental crisis is to praise God, for praising God is that act of worship and mode of existence that reminds us that we human beings are not free to do whatever our science and technology enable us to do. Praise flies in the face of our culture's tendency to unrestrained exploitation. Praise, as an act of worship and mode of existence, insists that human identity and destiny are incomprehensible apart from God's sovereignty. To attempt to forge an identity and a destiny apart from God, as Westermann suggests, "must disturb and finally destroy life itself."[13] Psalm 8 instructs us that to praise God is to live and to live is to praise God.

Psalm 8 belongs in the headlines and on the editorial page, and I'm encouraged to have seen it there at least once in recent years. In an editorial entitled "On the Edge of Heaven," the editors of the *St. Louis Post-Dispatch* began by quoting Ps. 8:3 and then went on to describe the discovery by astronomers of a distant force which seems to be attracting to itself the Milky Way and other galaxies. The editorial concludes:

> Scientists themselves seem star-struck by the massiveness of this discovery and admit it will only add to their already substantial difficulties in explaining the universe's mysteries. To the poets and the psalmists, the mystery is the same as it always has been:
> "What is man, that thou art mindful of him."[14]

By articulating the mystery of the human self and its place in a vast universe, Psalm 8 also functions effectively to call us to a decision of paramount importance for our time and place. Can we, will we exercise God-given dominion toward the ends of happiness and life, or will we be agents of death and destruction? Psalm 8 is a call to life lived in openness to God's instruction and under God's sovereignty.

PSALM 8, THE BOOK OF JOB, AND THE NEW TESTAMENT

In recent years, biblical scholars have begun to realize that an interpretation of a text is not complete without a consideration of its contexts. In the case of Psalm 8, its immediate literary context raises a crucial interpretative question: How can the psalmist talk about the "glory and honor" of humanity when the immediately preceding psalms have described human beings who are "in distress" (4:1); whose "honor suffer[s] shame" (4:2);[15] who are "groaning" (5:1, RSV); who are "languishing," "sorely troubled," "weary," and "weak" (6:2-7,

RSV); who are pursued and threatened (7:1-2)? In short, what do we make of the identity of a creature who both suffers miserably and yet is "a little lower than God" (8:5)?

We shall address these questions more thoroughly in chapter 5, but at this point, it is appropriate to broaden our view from the immediate literary context to the larger canonical context, for the interpretive questions raised by the immediate context of Psalm 8 are dealt with most fully in the book of Job. Not surprisingly, the book of Job, like Psalm 8, clearly recalls the language of Genesis 1.[16] And the book of Job alludes frequently to Psalm 8.[17] The first and most obvious instance is in Job's first response to one of his three friends. After citing humanity's "hard service on earth" (7:1) and his own "emptiness" and "misery" (7:3), Job picks up the central question of Psalm 8 and turns it upside down:

> What are human beings, that you
>   make so much of them,
>   that you set your mind on them. . . ?
> (Job 7:17)

In short, Job asks the question of identity. The book of Job thus becomes an exploration of God's identity and purpose for humanity and an exploration of how the weak, suffering human creature can be "crowned . . . with glory and honor" and exercise the God-given vocation of "dominion." In chapter 7, Job obviously thinks Psalm 8 is simply wrong. Humanity has no "glory and honor"; humans are in no position to exercise dominion. By the end of the book, however, Job has changed his mind. His transformation occurs gradually and is finally evident in 42:6, which Gerald Janzen translates as follows:

> therefore I dissolve [i.e. I give up my former opinion],
> and change my mind about dust and ashes.[18]

Compare the traditional translation:

> "therefore I despise myself,
>   and repent in dust and ashes." (RSV, NRSV)

Several considerations commend Janzen's translation. The Hebrew verb in 42:6*a* (*m's*) has no direct object; the "myself" is supplied by translators. This verb is ambiguous, but Janzen's "dissolve" makes more sense of the text than the traditional "despise." Furthermore, *nhm* in 42:6*b* frequently means "repent," not in the sense of repenting from sin but simply in the sense of changing one's mind. It is in this sense that God repents in Exodus 32:12, 14; Jonah 3:9-10; 4:2; and Amos 7:3, 6. Moreover, in terms of the plot of the book of Job, Job does not need to repent of sin. The whole plot turns on the assumption that Job has done nothing wrong to deserve his suffering. Finally, "dust and ashes" elsewhere in the book of Job is a designation for frail humanity (30:19; see Gen. 18:27). In short, Job has changed his mind about frail, weak, suffering humanity; he has changed his mind about Psalm 8. Suffering is not incompatible with "glory and honor." Beginning with a reference to Psalm 8, Janzen sums up the message of the book of Job as follows:

The Israelite vision of humankind—of *'adam*, the earthling— came to one kind of expression in Genesis 1 and 2, as well as in Psalm 8. On the one hand Job's experience caused him to question and to doubt that vision (cf. e.g., 29:25; 19:9; 30:19; and 7:17-18 with Ps. 8). On the other hand, in spite of his despair concerning the implications of his experience, not only for himself but also for humankind as a whole (7:17-18), he repeatedly returned to such affirmations as those in 23:10 (cf. 22:23-25) and 31:35-37. . . .

In the latter alternative, self-understanding as "dust and ashes," with all the suffering to which it is vulnerable, is not incompatible with royal status [the "glory and honor" and "dominion" of Psalm 8] but now may be accepted as the very condition under which royalty manifests itself. Henceforth, to affirm oneself as "dust and ashes" *need* not be an act of self-abasement . . . an affirmation of oneself as "dust and ashes" may also become an act in which the royal vocation of humanity—the royal vocation to *become* humanity—is accepted and embraced with all its vulnerability to innocent suffering.[19]

Janzen's reading of the book of Job enables us to make sense of the juxtaposition of Psalms 4–7 and Psalm 8. The "glory and honor" of humanity (Psalm 8) are not incompatible with the distress, trouble, and weakness of humanity portrayed in Psalms 4–7. This instruction about human identity is congruent with the conclusion drawn in chapter 1; that is, to be "righteous" does not exempt one from suffering. The psalms of lament or complaint will reinforce this conclusion (see chap. 5).

The book of Psalms and the book of Job also have profound implications for understanding the identity of God. If humanity is in the "image of God,"[20] then God too shares in the distress and suffering of the creation and the human creature. As Janzen suggests, an "act of completion" is required by the reader of the book of Job; and Janzen's approach to Job points toward the New Testament, especially to texts such as Mark 10:35-45; Matthew 16:13-28; Philippians 2:5-11; and Colossians 1:15-20. In each of these texts, the one who is recognized as the complete embodiment of God, the perfect image of God, is the one who serves by suffering.[21]

In this light, the quotation of Psalm 8:4-6 in Hebrews 2:9 does not seem nearly as arbitrary as some commentators have assumed.[22] At first sight it appears that the author of Hebrews read the Hebrew "son of man" (8:5; NRSV, "mortals") as a christological title and interpreted the phrase as a reference to Jesus. While this indeed may have been the case, this is not a necessary conclusion, nor does the theological argument depend on this conclusion. Rather, the author of Hebrews uses Psalm 8 to portray Jesus as the representative of all humanity, the authentic human being. Jesus' suffering is not incompatible with his glory and honor (Heb. 2:9). In making this affirmation, the author of Hebrews addresses the same theological question posed by the juxtaposition of Psalms 4–7 and Psalm 8. And ultimately, his affirmation about divine and human identity is in keeping with that articulated by the book of Job. Jesus is the one who makes it clear that the glory of God (Heb. 1:3-4) is not incompatible with human suffering and that the suffering of humanity does not exempt humanity from sharing in the glory of God (2:10-18; note the repetition of "glory" in 1:3 and 2:10). In short, both the immediate literary context and the *larger* canonical context of Psalm 8 give an added dimension to the psalm's call to decision. Psalm 8 is a call to life lived in openness to God's instruction and under God's sovereignty; that is, it is a call to exercise "dominion over . . . all things" (8:6) as a suffering servant.

PSALM 100

Psalm 100 is perhaps the most well-known hymn or song of praise. As Mays suggests: "Were the statistics known, Psalm 100 would probably prove to be the song most often chanted from within the history that runs from the Israelite temple on Mount Zion to the synagogues and churches spread across the earth."[23]

Psalm 100 is certainly *the* hymn of the Reformed tradition. A metrical version of the psalm, "All People That on Earth Do Dwell" was composed by William Kethe, a friend of John Knox, in 1561. The tune of Louis Bourgeois became known as "Old Hundredth," even though it was originally composed for a paraphrase of Psalm 134.[24] "Old Hundredth" is now the tune that accompanies words that many Christian congregations know simply as "The Doxology" (literally, "the word of glory/praise"). Thus it is appropriate that we use Psalm 100 to conclude this chapter. It also provides an overview and summary of what the Psalms teach about praise and identity.

To be noted first of all is the addressee of the summons to praise in verse 1, "all the earth." The songs of praise in the Psalter stop at nothing short of universality. They impel God's people toward the transcendence of barriers that divide people and diminish God's intent for humanity and all creation. Israel's story of God's dealing with the world began with the creation of 'ādām, "humanity." Even when the focus of the story narrows to one family, Abraham and Sarah, the narrator cannot manage to confine God's concern to anything less than all humanity. Abram, "exalted father" of Israel, becomes Abraham, "ancestor of a multitude of nations" (Gen. 17:5).

Furthermore, it has been clear from the beginning of Abram's story that the blessing he is promised is somehow intended for "all the families of the earth" (Gen. 12:3). To summon any congregation less than "all the earth" is to misunderstand the identity of the God of Israel and the God of Jesus Christ.

To be noted second is the imperative that continues the summons to praise in verse 2: "Serve the LORD" (RSV). The Hebrew word translated here as "serve" (*'bd*) can mean "worship," but to render this phrase "Worship the LORD" (NRSV) does not satisfactorily convey the comprehensiveness of the term. To "serve" means to orient one's whole life and existence to a sovereign master—literally, to be the "servant" or "slave" of a king. The term always occurs in the Psalter in relation to a royal figure, either human or divine.[25] The imagery of royalty also includes the imperatives "make a joyful noise" and "come into his presence"; both phrases elsewhere describe behavior toward human kings (1 Kings 1:28, 32; 1 Sam. 10:24). The inseparability of service and kingship is also clear in other contexts. The culminating affirmation of the people following their deliverance from the Egyptians is, "The LORD will reign forever and ever" (Exod. 15:18). This proclamation of the Lord's kingship is especially appropriate, for the stated goal of the exodus is that the Lord's people may "serve" the Lord (Exod. 4:23; 7:16; 8:20; 9:1, 13; 10:3; see also 12:31). Service and kingship belong together. It is perhaps not coincidental that one of the only two occurrences in the Psalter of the phrase "serve the LORD" occurs in Psalm 100:2, immediately following Psalms 93–99, which proclaim and celebrate the Lord's kingship. Interestingly, the other occurrence is in Psalm 2:11, suggesting that Psalm 100 and the other songs of praise are fundamentally about what Psalm 2 affirms the whole Psalter is about—the reign of God (see chap. 2).

To be noted third is the imperative that begins verse 3. Indeed, Psalm 100 is structured in such a way that one will especially notice verse 3. Whereas there is a series of three imperatives in verses 1-2 and 4, the variation of this pattern in verse 3 adds emphasis to the imperative "know." Furthermore, the lone imperative in verse 3 is of a different order; it demands not that the reader act but that the reader "know" something that will underlie all action. In short, while other hymns or songs of praise are implicitly instructional, Psalm 100 explicitly intends to teach. And, not surprisingly, the lesson is about the identity of God and humanity. A literal translation of the verse makes the nature of the teaching even clearer:

> Know that Yahweh, he [is] God.
> He made us, and not we,
> his people and the sheep of his pasture.

As Mays points out, verse 3 is a variation on what Walter Zimmerli identified as the "recognition formula" ("and you will know that I am Yahweh"), which elsewhere always follows a description of Yahweh's activity.[26] Here the imperative, "Know that Yahweh, he [is] God," introduces a description of God's activity: "He made us." There is a rich ambiguity present in the word translated "made." It could refer to God's creation of the world and all living things, or it could refer to the "making" or election of Israel as God's own people.[27] In all likelihood, the ambiguity is intentional; Israel could never tell the story of its election apart from an understanding of God's intention for "all the earth" (v. 1). The reasons for praise in verse 5 also point in both directions. "Good" is reminiscent of the recurring evaluation of God's creative acts in Genesis 1, whereas "steadfast love" and "faithfulness" recall God's self-revelation to Moses in Exodus 34 (see above on Psalm 117). The identity of Israel and all humanity is incomprehensible apart from God.

The focus on identity is reinforced by other stylistic features of Psalm 100. For instance, the personal name for God, "Yahweh," occurs four times in this short psalm, as if to emphasize that the identity of God is of paramount concern. Furthermore, the clustering of personal pronouns and pronominal suffixes in verse 3 is striking, as is their sequence: "he . . . he . . . us . . . we . . . his . . . his." This chiastic arrangement suggests dramatically that the question of human identity must begin and end with an understanding of God's identity. Human life is incomprehensible simply in reference to itself. In a quite different context, the apostle Paul taught the Corinthians the same lesson: "Or do you not *know* that your body is a temple of the Holy Spirit within you, which you have from God, and that *you are not your own?* For you were bought with a price; therefore *glorify God* in your body" (1 Cor. 6:19-20, emphasis added). As Paul knew, we are not our own; therefore, the only proper response is to "glorify God."

To be noted finally is that the concluding imperatives in verse 4 point to the very same conclusion. "Thanksgiving" and "praise" become the mode of existence that characterizes those who know that they belong to God, who know that they are not and can never be simply "self-made" men and women. To live is to praise God, and to praise God is to live. Or as Westermann put it, to praise anything or anyone other than God "must disturb and finally destroy life itself."[28]

Psalm 100 is in the final analysis, therefore, an "act of sanity," as Brueggemann calls it:

> Obviously our world is at the edge of insanity and we with it. Inhumaneness is developed as a scientific enterprise. Greed is celebrated as economic advance. Power runs unbridled to destructiveness.
>
> In a world like this one, our psalm is an act of sanity, whereby we may be "reclothed in our rightful minds" (cf. Mark 5:15). . . . Life is no longer self-grounded without thanks but rooted in thanks.[29]

Brueggemann cites Geoffrey Wainwright, who has pointed out what is undoubtedly true: "The world is not an easy place in which to live doxologically."[30] Walker Percy makes essentially the same observation. In addressing the question of why "Most People Have So Much Trouble Living in the Ordinary World,"[31] Percy suggests that for the most part, "scientists and artists and the autonomous self have gotten rid of God."[32] This is why it is so difficult to live "doxologically"; or as Percy puts it, to live "under the direct sponsorship of God, is a difficult if not nigh-impossible task."[33] This is true even for religious persons. Half-jokingly and half-seriously, Percy describes the faithful as "obnoxious," but the real threat to human life is the "autonomous self":

> Question: Who is the most obnoxious, Protestants, Catholics, or Jews?
> Answer: It depends on where you are and who you are talking to—though it is hard to conceive any one of the three consistently outdoing the other two in obnoxiousness. Yet, as obnoxious as are all three, none is as murderous as the autonomous self who, believing in nothing, can fall prey to ideology and kill millions of people—unwanted people, old people, sick people, useless people, unborn people, enemies of the state—and do so reasonably, without passion.[34]

As difficult as it may be in our world, to live "doxologically" is of paramount importance, for to praise anything or anyone other than God "must disturb and finally destroy life itself." At this point, the hymns or songs of praise offer the same instruction as Psalm 1. To be "wicked" is essentially to be an autonomous self, and "a wicked life leads only to ruin" (Ps. 1:6).[35] As Percy aptly notes, Flannery O'Connor is one writer who has managed the difficult task of living and working "under the direct sponsorship of God."[36] Indeed, O'Connor's short story entitled "Revelation" illustrates masterfully what praise is about. Most of the story takes place in a doctor's waiting room, where Mrs. Turpin, the main character, reflects upon and discusses how thankful she is that she is not like other classes of people. In horror Mrs. Turpin contemplates the almost unthinkable: "What if Jesus had said, 'All right, you can be white-trash or a nigger or ugly!' "[37]

A turning point in the story comes when an ugly girl in the waiting room goes out of her mind and suddenly attacks Mrs. Turpin, telling her, "Go back to hell where you came from, you old wart hog."

This "revelation" unsettles Mrs. Turpin, and she spends the rest of the day contemplating what it means. Toward evening, as she is cleaning out the hog pen, Mrs. Turpin speaks aloud her thoughts, addressing them to God.: " 'How am I a hog?' she demanded. 'Exactly how am I like them?' . . . A final surge of fury shook her and she roared, 'Who do you think you are?' "[38]

These are the last words Mrs. Turpin speaks, and quite tellingly they raise the issue of identity: Who is she? Who is God? She is now ready for another revelation as she stares at the pigs, who "had settled all in one corner around the old sow who was grunting softly." This scene becomes the clue to the revelation that ends the story and illustrates so marvelously what the songs of praise intend to teach. When Mrs. Turpin lifts her head from the hog pen, after "absorbing some abysmal life-giving knowledge," the sight of a purple streak in the sky becomes a further revelation:

> A visionary light settled in her eyes. She saw the streak as a vast swinging bridge extending upward from the earth through a field of living fire. Upon it a vast horde of souls were rumbling toward heaven. There were whole companies of white-trash, clean for the first time in their lives, and bands of black niggers in white robes, and battalions of freaks and lunatics shouting and clapping and leaping like frogs. And bringing up the end of the procession was a tribe of people whom she recognized at once as those who, like herself and Claud [her husband], had always had a little of everything and the God-given wit to use it right. She leaned forward to observe them closer. They were marching behind the others with great dignity, accountable as they had always been for good order and common sense and respectable behavior. They alone were on key. Yet she could see by their shocked and altered faces that even their virtues were being burned away. . . . In a moment the vision faded but she remained where she was, immobile.
> At length she got down and turned off the faucet and made her slow way on the darkening path back to the house. In the woods around her the invisible cricket choruses had struck up, but what she heard were the voices of the souls climbing upward into the starry field and shouting hallelujah.[39]

The "life-giving knowledge," the instruction, which Mrs. Turpin received was nothing less than an understanding of what Psalm 100:1 means by "Make a joyful noise to the LORD, *all the earth.*" It means understanding that the people "accountable . . . for good order and common sense and respectable behavior" really do not rule the world after all. It is God who reigns. It means the transcendence of barriers as all classes of people, indeed "all the earth," join together in making a joyful noise. It means that in the light of God's acceptance of and enduring love for "all the earth," we finally understand who we are as we see even our "virtues . . . being burned away." Given the nature of this instruction, this "life-giving knowl-edge," it is appropriate that the final word Mrs. Turpin hears is "hallelujah." It is the final word of Flannery O'Connor's story, and it is the final word of the Psalter (150:6): "Praise the LORD."

Where the Psalter ends, life begins. To praise God is to live, and to live is to praise God. Because the Reformed tradition has so treasured Psalm 100, it is fitting that its essential in-struction about praise and identity be contained in the first question and answer of the Westminster Shorter Catechism:

Question: What is the chief end of humanity?
Answer: Humanity's chief end is to glorify God and enjoy God forever.

CHAPTER 4

PRAISE AND ACTIVITY: WHO SHALL ASCEND THE HILL OF THE LORD?

The preceding chapter has already suggested that praise involves "activity" as well as "identity." Indeed, it is impossible and undesirable to separate these concepts too sharply. Obviously, who we are and what we do are inevitably and inextricably related, as Psalms 8 and 100 recognized. In Psalm 8, the question of identity ("What are human beings. . . ?"; v. 4) is answered at least partly in terms of the activity of "dominion" (v. 6). In Psalm 100, the imperative "serve" (v. 2; NRSV "worship") calls for the orientation of one's whole life, doing as well as being, to God's reign.

In a sense, then, this chapter will say nothing new when it speaks of praise in terms of "activity." Nevertheless, since "identity" and "activity" are often distinguished conceptually, it is important not to ignore a psalm that answers the question of identity ("Who. . . ?"; Ps. 24:3) specifically in terms of activity. Psalm 24 affirms that belonging to God involves a certain activity or style of life. This chapter will conclude with an interpretation of Psalm 113, which focuses almost entirely on God's activity. In so doing, it reminds us of something we are frequently inclined to forget—namely, our human activity is grounded in God's activity on our behalf.

PSALM 24

Earlier generations of scholars often concluded that Psalm 24 is composed of three liturgical fragments (vv. 1-2, 3-6, 7-10), but the recent consensus favors the unity of the psalm.[1] This unity that scholars detect, however, is the unity of a liturgical ceremony, such as a processional of worshipers accompanying the ark into the Temple area. Verses 1-2, for instance, consist of an opening profession of faith by the worshipers; verses 3-6 consist of an exchange between worshipers (v. 3) and priests (vv. 4-6) concerning who may enter the sanctuary; and verses 7-10 consist of a responsorial liturgy that takes place as the processional prepares to enter the gates of the Temple area. H. J. Kraus summarizes this point of view when he concludes that Psalm 24 consists of "individual pieces of a liturgy that accompanies the cultic act of bringing in the ark at the sanctuary."[2]

In short, form critics classify Psalm 24 as an "entrance liturgy." Considerable disagreement surrounds the question of the precise cultic setting in which this liturgy may have been used. Some have proposed the existence of an autumn New Year festival to celebrate annually the enthronement of Yahweh.[3] Other scholars have suggested an annual festival to celebrate the Lord's choice of David and Zion (see 2 Samuel 6–7; Psalm 132). More recently, it has been proposed that "Psalm 24 has to do with some ritual celebrated at the second temple (see Ezekiel 43-44), the coming of Yahweh into his sanctuary, and his passing through heavily guarded temple gates," or perhaps an "even more symbolic enactment of such a coming in a templeless, synagogual environment."[4]

To be sure, several of the above hypotheses are plausible. Perhaps more than any other psalm, Psalm 24 allows the interpreter to imagine a liturgical ceremony or procession in which the psalm could have been used. Even so, the identification of Psalm 24 as an "entrance liturgy" and the attempt to identify its liturgical setting do not deal adequately with the content and theology of the psalm. The following observation by R. A. F. Mackenzie is pertinent: "The psalm is a beautiful poetic-liturgical text, simple, stirring, and dramatic. It is also a *credo*, packed with doctrinal affirmations about God and [human] relationship to God."[5] In short, there is a unity of content and theology in Psalm 24 in addition to a unity associated with a particular liturgical ceremony.

When our attention is directed beyond questions of form and function to matters of content and theology, we notice that Psalm 24 addresses the same fundamental issues that we have already encountered in Psalms 1–2, 8, 19, 95–96, 100, 117, 119, and 150. For instance, the question of identity is explicit and paramount. Two questions about the identity of humans (v. 3) are matched by two questions about the identity of God (vv. 8, 10). Both the questions themselves as well as the answers focus our attention on what we have already identified as the central affirmation of the Psalter: The Lord reigns! The word *king* appears five times in verses 7-10; and other elements of the vocabulary of verses 7-10 also focus attention on God's reign. The adjective "strong" occurs elsewhere only in Isaiah 43:17, almost immediately following an affirmation of the Lord's kingship in Isaiah 43:15; and the related noun for "strength" is prominent in the psalms that proclaim the Lord's kingship (see Pss. 29:1; 93:1; 96:6-7; 99:4). The same can be said of the noun "glory" (*kābôd*, vv. 7, 8, 9, 10; see Pss. 29:1, 3, 9; 96:3, 7-8; 97:6, 145:11-12). The phrase "mighty in battle" (v. 8) recalls the description of the Lord as a "man of war" near the beginning of the Song of the Sea (Exod. 15:3), a song that concludes with the affirmation that "the Lord will reign forever and ever" (Exod. 15:18).

The identity of the Lord as king also provides the unifying link between verses 7-10 and verses 1-2. Although the word *king* does not appear in verses 1-2, these verses mention "the world" (*tēbēl*, v. 1) that the Lord has "established." These same two words and the same affirmation occur in Psalms 93:1; 96:10; both of these verses specifically affirm "the Lord is king." In short, verses 1-2 and verses 7-10 unite in proclaiming that the Lord reigns. And significantly, it is the proclamation of the Lord's reign that surrounds, both structurally and theologically, the question of the identity of humanity in verses

3-6. When the questions of verse 3 are heard in the context of verses 1-2, 7-10, these questions do not simply pose the issue of which worshipers may enter the Temple gates. Rather, the questions in verse 3 ask in effect: Who shall live under God's reign? Who shall enter the kingdom of God?

As suggested above, it is significant that the answer to these questions specifically involves a certain activity or style of life. In other words, ethics begins with the profession that God rules the world. The same understanding of the grounding of ethics in the reality of God's reign is found in the shape of the Pentateuch. Only after the delivered people have recognized and proclaimed God's reign (Exod. 15:18) does God give the commandments and receive the people's response: "All that the LORD has spoken we will do, and we will be obedient" (Exod. 24:7; see 24:3).

It is not surprising that Psalm 24:4 alludes to the Decalogue, which is the first of the series of commandments given at Sinai. For instance, three words in verse 4 also occur in the third commandment in Exodus 20:7. A literal translation of the two verses follows, with the repeated words italicized:

> (The one who has) *clean* [*nĕqî*, nominal form of the root *nqh*] hands and purity of heart,
> who (does) not *lift up* [*nāśā'*] to *nothingness* [*šāwĕ'*] his soul,
> and does not take an oath in deceit. (Ps. 24:4)
> You shall not *lift up* [*tiśśā'*, Qal imperfect of *nāśā'*] the name of the Lord your God to *nothingness* [*šāwĕ'*], for the Lord will not *hold clean* [*yĕnaqqeh*, piel imperfect of *nqh*] the one who *lifts up* [*yiśśā'*, Qal, imperfect of *nāśā'*] his name to *nothingness* [*šāwĕ'*]. (Exod. 20:7)

The noun *šāwĕ'* sometimes mean "nothingness" in the sense of "idol" (Ps. 31:7; Jer. 18:5). Thus both Exodus 20:7 and Psalm 24:4 affirm that "cleanness" results from nothing less than trusting the Lord completely and unreservedly. Interestingly, the idiom "to lift up the soul" occurs again at the very beginning of Psalm 25: "To you, O LORD, I lift up my soul." In this case and in the two other cases where the psalmist says she or he lifts up the soul to the Lord, the word *trust* (*bṭḥ*) occurs in the immediate context (see Pss. 25:1-2; 86:2, 4; 143:8). When the questions and answer of Psalm 24:3-4 are heard in the context of verses 1-2, 7-10, the message is this: Ethical behavior, every human choice and activity, is to be grounded in trusting God and in the reality of God's reign.

Commentators frequently point out that Psalm 24:4 does not indicate very specifically what kind of activity should be engaged in by those who "ascend the hill of the LORD" (v. 3), who enter the reign of God. "Clean hands" and "pure hearts" may be intended to indicate outward behavior and inward motivation respectively. The only other place in the Old Testament where the phrase "pure (of) heart" occurs is Psalm 73:1, where the parallel is "Israel." Perhaps not coincidentally, the psalmist also says in Psalm 73:13, "I have . . . washed my hands in innocence [*niqqāyôn*]," which is very similar to the "clean [*nĕqî*] hands" of Psalm 24:4. Psalm 73, however, offers no more indication than Psalm 24 of what specific activity is involved. What the psalmist does suggest is that if she or he did not wash her or his "hands in innocence," the psalmist would be forsaking the "circle [*dôr*] of your [God's] children" (73:15). Psalm 24:6 also concludes that "those who have clean hands and pure hearts" (v. 4) constitute "the company [*dôr*] of those who seek" God.

This lack of specificity, however, is theologically appropriate. What we are left with is the conclusion suggested above: Every human activity is to originate from trusting God completely, from living under God's reign, from understanding oneself as among "the company of those who seek" God (Ps. 24:6) and who are God's "children" (Ps. 73:15). Living under God's reign has never been, is not now, and will never be simply a matter of following a set of specific rules and regulations. To pretend that it is or could be is to open oneself to the most rigid kind of legalism, which results finally in reinforcing a particular status quo. It is interesting and revealing that all three psalms in which the psalmist says, "to you, O LORD, I lift up my soul" (Pss. 25:1; 86:4; see 143:8), the psalmist also specifically asks the Lord to "teach me" (Pss. 25:4-5; and see vv. 8-9, 12; 86:11; 143:8). Ethical activity begins with the affirmation that God rules the world (Ps. 24:1-2), and it inevitably involves the persistent posture of openness to God's instruction.

That ethical activity cannot be reduced to following a specific set of rules and regulations has been argued forcefully by Stanley Hauerwas and William H. Willimon: "So the primary ethical question is not, what ought I now to do? but rather, how does the world really look? . . . Our ethics derive from what we have seen of God."[6]

Psalm 24:1-2 is intended to answer this primary ethical question: How does the world really look?

> The earth is the LORD's and all that is in it,
>   the world, and those who live in it;
> for he has founded it on the seas,
>   and established it on the rivers.

In terms of what we ought now to do, Psalm 24 suggests that our every activity should follow from our trust that God rules the world (v. 4). Hauerwas and Willimon offer a challenge to the church, to the "company of those who seek" God (v. 6):

> We would like a church that again asserts that God, not nations, rules the world, that the boundaries of God's kingdom transcend those of Caesar's, and that the main political task of the church is the formation of a people who see clearly the cost of discipleship and are willing to pay the price.[7]

In this challenge, Hauerwas and Willimon are in agreement with Psalm 24. The most important political activity for the church is to tell persons "not [to] lift up their souls to what is false," and thus to form a people who trust God unreservedly and whose every activity is grounded in the reality of God's reign: "Such is the company of those who seek" God (24:6).

Hauerwas and Willimon's discussion of "The Church as a Basis for Christian Ethics" centers on the Sermon on the Mount (Matthew 5–7),[8] and given the agreement we have detected between their conclusions and Psalm 24, it is not surprising to discover that Psalm 24 has numerous points of contact with the Sermon on the Mount. As suggested above, Psalm 24:1-2, 7-10 unites in proclaiming God's reign. This same proclamation lies at the heart of the Sermon on the Mount. In Matthew, Jesus' proclamation of the kingdom of heaven is the announcement that God reigns; this announcement inaugurates Jesus' public ministry (4:17) and pervades the Sermon on the Mount. For instance, the first and last of what appear to be the original eight Beatitudes (Matt. 5:3-10; vv. 11-12 appear to be an expansion of v. 10, and v. 11 shifts from third to second person address) mention the kingdom of heaven, thus providing an *inclusio* for the series. In short, the proclamation of God's reign surrounds the Beatitudes, both structurally and theologically. The phrase "kingdom of heaven" also occurs twice in Matthew 5:17-20; and the phrase (or its equivalent, "kingdom of God") recurs throughout the Sermon on the Mount and throughout Jesus' teaching in the Synoptic Gospels.

In Psalm 24:5, those who trust God unreservedly and whose activity is grounded in the reality of God's reign "will receive blessing from the LORD, / and vindication from the God of their salvation." The Hebrew underlying the English "vindication" is *ṣĕdāqâ*, usually translated "righteousness." Psalm 24 thus characterizes life under God's rule with the concepts of "blessing" and "righteousness," and so does the Sermon on the Mount. Each of the Beatitudes begins with "Blessed," and the concept of "righteousness" is central to both the Beatitudes and the entire Sermon. The original eight Beatitudes are often divided into two smaller series of four, verses 3-6 and verses 7-10. The final verse of each series contains the word *righteousness*. The context in Matthew also emphasizes the importance of the concept. According to Jesus in Matthew 3:15, his baptism was "to fulfill all righteousness." In 5:17-20, which many scholars suggest is the key to understanding the Sermon on the Mount, Jesus says that "unless your righteousness exceeds that of the scribes and Pharisees, you will never enter the kingdom of heaven" (5:20; see also 6:33). In short, conventional good behavior, following all the rules and regulations, is not sufficient in God's reign: "You have heard that it was said to those of ancient times. . . . But I say to you . . . " (Matt. 5:21-22; see vv. 27-28, 33-34, 38-39, 43-44). The greater righteousness is not primarily a matter of asking "What ought I now to do?" Rather, it is fundamentally a matter of asking, "How does the world really look?" For Psalm 24 and for Jesus, the world appears as the sphere of God's reign. The psalm and the Sermon on the Mount unite in affirming that "our ethics derive from what we have seen of God."[9]

Indeed, one of the Beatitudes speaks specifically in terms of seeing God: "Blessed are the pure in heart, for they will see God" (Matt. 5:8). Again, the similarity to Psalm 24 is clear. Those who enter the reign of God are those "who have clean hands and *pure hearts*" (v. 4; emphasis added); it is they "who *seek the face* of the God of Jacob" (v. 6; emphasis added). In Exodus 33:17-23, seeing the face of God is prohibited; even Moses can only see God's back. Thus it is rather extraordinary for Psalm 24:6 to speak of those who "seek the face of the God of Jacob" and for Matthew 5:8 to speak about those who "will see God." What a monumental experience is in view—indeed, nothing short of the creation of a new world that turns the current world upside down (see Acts 17:6). Such is the import of Psalm 24 and the Sermon on the Mount, both of which invite persons to enter the extraordinary new world of God's reign.

Much of what Jack Kingsbury says of the Sermon on the Mount applies also to Psalm 24:

> Matthew refuses to make the reality of sin and little faith the determining factor in his ethic. Instead, the determining factor for him is the reality of God's eschatological kingdom, or rule, which is present even now in the earthly and risen Jesus Son of God. For disciples who live in the sphere where God rules through the risen Jesus, doing the greater righteousness is the normal order of things.[10]

As for Matthew, the "determining factor" for Psalm 24 is "the reality of God's eschatological kingdom." Like the Sermon on the Mount and like Psalm 2 (see chap. 2), Psalm 24 is eschatological. When read and heard in its literary context, it calls for a decision: Who is sovereign (vv. 8, 10)? Who rules the world? Who shall enter the reign of God (v. 3)?

The church traditionally uses Psalm 24 during the season of Advent. This season is not primarily a time of preparation to celebrate again the birth of Jesus. Rather, it focuses attention on Christ's coming again and on "the reality of God's eschatological kingdom, or rule, which is present even now in the earthly and risen Jesus Son of God." Advent, the first season of the Christian year, calls for a decision that is fundamental for all seasons. Psalm 24 is indeed an Advent psalm, because it affirms the reality of God's reign and invites persons to live under God's rule. For those who see the world as the sphere of God's reign, every ethical decision, every human activity, will be grounded in and result from unreserved trust in God and in the reality of God's reign.

PSALM 113

Psalm 113 is a hymn (see chap. 3) that, as Peter Craigie points out, has been given by Jews and Christians "a special place in their repertoire of praise."[11] The psalm traditionally belongs to the celebrations of Passover and Easter. As in the other hymns we have examined, the question of identity is paramount in Psalm 113. For instance, each of the first three verses contains the word *name;* especially in ancient cultures, names were intended to convey the essence, reality, or identity of a person. Each of the first five verses of the psalm contains the divine name "Yahweh," culminating in verse 5, which explicitly poses the question of identity: "Who is like the LORD our God. . . ?" Verse 5 happens to be the central line of the psalm. Everything prior to verse 5 builds up to the central question of identity, and beginning with verse 5*b*, everything following is intended to answer the central question.

After verse 5*a*, there is no further occurrence of the word *name*, nor do verses 5*b*-9 contain a divine name, with the exception of the final invitation to praise (that is, *hallelu-yah*, in which the element *yah* is a shortened form of the divine name

Yahweh). Instead, God's identity is described in terms of God's activity. Each of the six verbal forms in verses 5*b*-9 are what is known in Hebrew as the *hiphil;* it is a causative form of the verb. A more literal translation captures the effect: God "makes high in order to sit" (v. 5*b*); God "makes low in order to see" (v. 6*a*); God "causes the poor to arise" (v. 7*a*); God "makes exalted the needy . . . to cause them to sit with princes" (vv. 7*b*-8*a*); God "makes to dwell" (v. 9*a*). In short, God is active; God makes things happen.

There are several other interesting aspects to this description of God's activity. One involves the imagery of high and low. While God is "high [*rām*] above all nations" (v. 4) and "seated on high," God "makes [God's self] low in order to look upon heaven and upon earth" (v. 6; my translation). There are immediate consequences of God's apparent self-abasement. God "raises [*hiphil* participle of *qûm*] the poor from the dust, and lifts [*hiphil* imperfect of *rûm*] the needy from the ash heap" (v. 7). The repetition of the root *rûm* in verses 4 and 7 is particularly revealing: the exalted one has chosen to be humbled, and the humbled are thus exalted.

Another noteworthy aspect of the description of God's activity is the repetition of the Hebrew root *yšb*, "to sit, to live, to dwell." God, who dwells or "is *seated* on high" (v. 5*b*), makes the needy dwell or "*sit* with princes" (v. 8*b*) and, according to a literal translation of verse 9*a*, God "*makes to dwell* the barren of home" (NRSV = "gives the barren woman a home"). Again, the exalted God is involved in the activity of exalting the humbled.

The description of God's activity in Psalm 113 is markedly similar to the language of two other biblical songs—the Song of Hannah in 1 Samuel 2:2-8 (cf. esp. Ps. 113:7-8 with 1 Sam. 2:8 and Ps. 113:9 with 1 Sam. 2:5) and Mary's song, the Magnificat, in Luke 1:46-55. Like Psalm 113, both these songs celebrate God's exaltation of those who are humbled (1 Sam. 2:4-5, 7-8; Luke 1:48, 51-53). All three of these songs tend to have special appeal to those Christians who, like myself, have been nurtured in the tradition loosely known as liberal Protestantism. One reason is clear. These texts provide support for the "peace with justice" stance of liberal Protestanism: God has a preferential option for the poor, and our calling is to work on behalf of the poor, the needy, the homeless.

So far, so good. Psalm 113 may indeed be legitimately interpreted as an invitation to join God at God's work in the world on behalf of the humbled. At the same time, however, Psalm 113 is a powerful warning against the temptation to which Protestant liberalism has often yielded—namely, the temptation to leave God out of the picture entirely. Willimon and Hauerwas state it well: "Most of our social activism is formed on the presumption that God is superfluous to the formation of a world of peace with justice. Fortunately, we are powerful people who, because we live in a democracy, are free to use power. It is all up to us."[12]

In short, the temptation is toward autonomy, to be "a law unto ourselves." Reinhold Niebuhr described the temptation over sixty years ago in his reflections on the American observance of the Thanksgiving holiday: "Thanksgiving becomes increasingly the business of congratulating the Almighty upon his most excellent co-workers, ourselves."[13]

The nature and subtlety of this temptation is portrayed movingly by Flannery O'Connor in her story "The Lame Shall Enter First." In the story, Sheppard, a well-intentioned City Recreation Director, goes to great lengths to assist a lame juvenile delinquent, Johnson. He takes the boy into his home, gets corrective shoes to offset the boy's condition, attempts to give him every possible advantage. In a conversation with Johnson, Sheppard's son Norton says of his father:

> "He's good," he mumbled. "He helps people."
> "Good!" Johnson said savagely. He thrust his head forward. "Listen here," he hissed. "I don't care if he's good or not. He ain't *right!*"[14]

What Johnson means becomes clear as the story unfolds. When Johnson refuses to cooperate easily with Sheppard's helpfulness, Sheppard initiates the following exchange:

> "I'm stronger than you are. I'm stronger than you are and I'm going to save you. The good will triumph."

"Not when it ain't true," the boy said, "Not when it ain't right."

"My resolve isn't shaken," Sheppard repeated. "I'm going to save you. . . . "

Johnson thrust his head forward. "Save yourself," he hissed. "Nobody can save me but Jesus."[15]

Johnson finally sums up Sheppard's motivation with the conclusion: "He thinks he's God."[16] Thus he illuminates the temptation to which Sheppard has yielded. For Sheppard, God was superfluous. In Sheppard's view, it was all up to himself. Thus his actions, well-intentioned as they were, were fundamentally selfish. He may have been good, but he wasn't right.

Likewise, the social activism of liberal Protestantism has often been good but not right, for it has frequently been fundamentally selfish. In seeking to save people, we have often made God superfluous, and not infrequently have impugned the integrity and freedom of those whom we have sought to help. Or we turn God into what Donald W. McCullough has called "the God-of-my-cause . . . [by] carving gods to fit the exact dimensions of our favorite ideologies." In the midst of this situation, McCullough suggests, "The time has come for a rediscovery of the transcendence of God."[17]

Psalm 113 is a powerful testimony to the transcendence of God (v. 5) and thus a powerful warning against the temptation to conclude, "It is all up to us." Psalm 113 affirms that God "raises the poor," God "lifts the needy," God "makes to dwell the barren of home." In short, God makes things happen. To be sure, we may, we must, join God at God's work in the world; but as Willimon and Hauerwas point out, "The moment that life is formed on the presumption that we are not participants in *God's* continuing history of creation and redemption, we are acting on unbelief rather than faith."[18]

In the final analysis, then, Psalm 113, like Psalm 24, affirms the reality of God's reign and invites persons to live under God's rule. Only when our activity is grounded in unreserved trust in God and in the reality of God's reign will it be possible to be both good and right. "Praise the LORD" (Ps. 113:1, 9)!

PART III:

INSTRUCTION FOR PRAYER AND PRAYER AS INSTRUCTION

CHAPTER 5

PRAYER AND IDENTITY: OUT OF THE DEPTHS

We began our consideration of the Psalter's instruction with "Instruction for Praise and Praise as Instruction," because praise is fundamental. It involves the affirmation of God's reign and the offering of the whole self to God. The prayers in the Psalter and the Psalter as a whole move toward praise (see chap. 3). While praise *is* fundamental, the voice of praise is *not* the dominant note in the book of Psalms. The hymns or songs of praise are outnumbered by prayers, more specifically, by prayers of lament or complaint.

Most people are surprised to learn this fact, because the church in recent years has done a remarkably thorough job of ignoring the psalms of lament. For instance, of the psalms printed as responsive readings in a widely used Presbyterian hymnal, the songs of praise or thanksgiving outnumber the laments by sixteen to six.[1] There are several reasons for this imbalance, but perhaps prime among them is the following one expressed by Brueggemann: "I think that serious religious use of the lament psalms has been minimal because we have believed that faith does not mean to acknowledge negativity."[2] As Brueggemann also points out, the church's loss of lament is "costly," psychologically, sociologically, and theologically. In psychological terms, the laments represent the believer's taking "initiative with God," thus avoiding the development

of a "false self" that simply accepts passively every circumstance that comes along. In sociological terms, the laments
represent the simple observation that "life isn't right," thus
raising the issue of justice and again avoiding a passivity that
simply accepts or reinforces the status quo. In theological
terms, the laments represent the conviction that God is not
"the silent *guarantor* of the status quo," but rather "God can be
addressed in risky ways as the *transformer* of what has not yet
appeared."[3]
   In short, like the hymns, the laments have much to teach us.
To be sure, as models of biblical prayer, they can teach us how
to pray. But in so doing, they also teach us about ourselves and
the world, as well as about God and how God rules the world.

PSALM 130

   In at least one important respect, Psalm 130 is the prototypical lament. Its opening words express the location or condition
from which all the laments arise: "Out of the depths." The
"depths" in this case have something to do with the psalmist's
own sinfulness (see chap. 6), but more often the experience of
the "depths" is precipitated by the psalmist's enemies (see
"deep waters" in Ps. 69:2, 14) or even by God. In any case, the
cries that come "out of the depths" are the psalmist's way of
saying, "Life isn't right."[4] What is of paramount importance,
however, is the psalmist's conviction that God is somehow
present in the depths, or at least within earshot: "Out of the
depths I cry *to you*, O Lord!"[5] This conviction lies at the very
heart of Israel's faith. The exodus, the central saving event of
the Old Testament, is described as being evoked by the people's crying out to God (see Exod. 3:7, 9); and the prophet of
the exile recalls the crossing of the sea as follows (Isa. 51:10):

> Was it not you [God] . . .
> who made the *depths* of the sea a way
> for the redeemed to cross over?

Nothing—neither "height, nor depth" (Rom. 8:39)—can separate God's people from the love of God.

In this regard, it is revealing that the Psalter's prototypical lament highlights precisely the same thing that is highlighted by the Psalter's prototypical song of praise, Psalm 117—namely, God's "steadfast love" (*hesed*; Pss. 117:2; 130:7). In fact, like Psalm 117 (see chap. 3) the vocabulary of Psalm 130 recalls God's self-revelation in Exodus 34. With God there is "forgiveness" (Ps. 130:4; Exod. 34:9; NRSV "pardon") of "iniquities" (Ps. 130:3, 8; Exod. 34: 7, 9, although the word is singular), which is manifestation of God's "steadfast love" (Ps. 130:7; Exod. 34:6-7). What Israel joyfully celebrated in songs of praise, Israel also appealed to "out of the depths"—God's *hesed,* God's "loyal love." At this point, what started as a prayer becomes a proclamation of good news (vv. 7-8). God's presence and power will be experienced not only upon the mountaintop but also in the darkest of the depths—even upon a cross!

The power of this gospel and this psalm has been evident through the centuries. One of Martin Luther's most well-known hymns is his metrical version of Psalm 130. Another of the early Reformers, Theodore Beza, is said to have died with the words of Psalm 130 upon his lips.[6] It is also said that John Wesley, the founder of Methodism, heard Psalm 130 performed as an anthem on May 24, 1738, at St. Paul's Cathedral. According to R. F. Prothero, "The Psalm was one of the influences that attuned his heart to receive that assurance of his salvation by faith, which the evening of the some day brought to him in the room at Aldersgate Street."[7] By Wesley's own account, his heart was "strangely warmed," not unlike perhaps those two disciples on the Emmaus road, who had their "hearts burning within" them as Jesus interpreted to them what was written about him "in the law of Moses, the prophets, and the psalms" (Luke 24:32, 44).

This is not to say that the Psalms are predictions of Jesus, but the laments certainly do testify to and instruct us about a God whose presence in the depths would ultimately be expressed by the death of God's Son on a cross. Not surprisingly, the

Gospel writers could not narrate the story of Jesus' suffering apart from the Psalms, especially Psalms 22 and 69 (which interestingly is the only other psalm that contains the word translated "depths," which the NRSV translates as "deep waters" in vv. 2 and 14; see the conclusion of this book for further discussion of these psalms). The laments have the capability to articulate the good news of a God who makes God's own self present in the depths. This capability alone explains why the loss of the laments is so "costly."

But beyond this capability, the laments offer to the righteous the language to address to God the reality that "life isn't right." This reality is not a temporary one. It is *always* the case that "life isn't right." And yet, the Psalms speak repeatedly of "the righteous," those "in the *right*." This is not a contradiction in terms. As suggested in chapter 1, to be righteous is to trust God—to be open to God's instruction, to live in dependence upon God. Thus while "life isn't right," *we* may be "in the right"/"righteous" not by our own accomplishments or wills, but by finding our refuge in God (Ps. 2:12). This message about the identity of God and humankind is reinforced by the shape of the Psalter and the shape of particular psalms of lament or complaint. To illustrate further, we turn to Psalms 3 and 13.

PSALM 3

As pointed out from the beginning, the shape of the Psalter is significant. Thus it makes sense to pay particular attention to the movement from Psalms 1–2, which introduce the Psalter, to Psalm 3 and beyond. As suggested in chapter 1, the psalmist is not a naive optimist; he or she knows what the "real world" is like. The transition from Psalms 1–2 to Psalm 3 removes any doubt about that, for Psalm 3:1-2 very explicitly locates the psalmist in the midst of a situation in which "life isn't right":

> O LORD, how many are my foes!
> Many are rising against me;

> many are saying to me,
> "There is no help for you in God."

The repetition of "many" drives home the point. The psalm-ist's problems are abundant. Indeed, the title of Psalm 3 has already linked the psalm to a terribly threatening and trying time in the life of David, "when he fled from his son Absalom." This notice should not be understood as historical. Rather, it invites the reader to consider David's predicament as illustra-tive of where we human beings regularly find ourselves.[8] David's family and administration were in shambles. Absalom had already killed his brother Amnon for raping his sister Tamar (2 Samuel 13). No sooner had David forgiven the be-loved Absalom (2 Samuel 14) than Absalom rebeled and drove his father in humiliation from Jerusalem (2 Samuel 15). What a mess! Life isn't right!

The movement from Psalms 1–2 to Psalm 3 suggests that blessedness/happiness (1:1; 2:12) and prosperity (1:3) will be experienced precisely in the midst of such a mess. For those of us who know predicaments like David's—violence, family turmoil, the agony of loving rebellious children, threats to life and livelihood—that is good news. "The way of the righteous" is not a detour around the trials and troubles of life; it is the trust that God is walking with us. God is present in the depths! And even there, precisely there, God makes life possible.[9]

This good news, this faith, this trust is certainly not the prevailing cultural creed. The foes of the psalmist voice what could well be the *credo* of our secular society: "There is no help for you in God." Or, more commonly put, "God helps those *who help themselves.*" When it gets right down to it, most of us, even most of us within the church, believe that "it is all up to us."[10]

But not the psalmist! The psalmist trusts that God helps those who *cannot* help themselves. The psalmist's concluding *credo* is the precise opposite of what the foes have affirmed. The psalmist says, "Help [NRSV, "deliverance"; but the He-brew word is essentially the same in vv. 2 and 8, *yĕšû â/ yĕšû ātâ*] belongs to the Lord" (my translation). And his prayer in verse 7 had appealed to the one whom the enemies had impugned. "Help me [*hôšî ʿēnî*; NRSV "Deliver me"], *O my God!*" The laments offer a thoroughly theological understanding of reality. There is ultimately no "help" for humankind apart from God (Ps. 3:7-8); there is no "hope" for individuals except in God (Ps. 130:5, 7).

This theological comprehension of reality is a challenge to us who live in a world that promotes autonomy—self-rule, self-reliance, self-help. As suggested in chapters 2 and 3, the affirmation of God's rule calls for a decision. Concerning the enemies' accusation in Psalm 3:2, "There is no help for you in God," Mays comments:

> One can either believe it—or believe in God. The psalm is composed to encourage faith and give it language. . . . It recites the doctrine that "salvation [or "help"; NRSV "deliverance"] belongs to the Lord" to remind the distressed that no trouble is beyond help and no human hostility can limit God's help. In all these ways, the psalm encourages and supports faith and invites the distressed to pray, the ultimate act of faith in the face of assault on the soul.[11]

Prayer is a way of life! This may sound as naive as the suggestion that was made in chapter 3 on the basis of Psalm 8—that is, the first step in addressing the environmental crisis is to praise God. But the alternative to praise and prayer is the pervasive conviction that "it is all up to us." The psalmists never believed that! Nor did the apostle Paul, who calls believers to unceasing prayer and praise: "Rejoice always, pray without ceasing, give thanks in all circumstances; for this is the will of God in Christ Jesus for you" (1 Thess. 5:16-18).

PSALM 13: PRAYER AND IDENTITY

In only six verses, Psalm 13 portrays the essential structure and movement of the laments. We shall examine it in more detail to explore further the issues raised by Psalms 3 and 130 and to formulate more explicitly what the laments teach us about prayer and the identity of God and humankind.

Verses 1-4

Psalm 13 falls neatly into three brief sections. Verses 1-2 are the lament or complaint proper. The most obvious feature is the four-fold repetition of "How long." The repetition serves both to emphasize the psalmist's impatience (as in the fourth or fortieth, "How long until we get there, Mommy?") and the growing urgency of the situation. As Robert Alter suggests, each repetition "reflects an ascent on a scale of intensity, the note of desperate urgency pitched slightly higher with each repetition."[12] It seems at first that God may have forgotten. No, God has positively turned away, hidden from the psalmist. Verse 2 describes the result—intense inner turmoil (the Hebrew of v. 2*a* reads literally "How long must I hold counsel in my soul") and "sorrow in my heart," which is elsewhere associated with the death of individuals (Gen. 42:38; 44:31) or the death of the nation (Jer. 8:18). The situation is urgent, a matter of life and death. The crowning ignominy is that in the midst of the psalmist's trouble, his or her enemy is "exalted," a position properly reserved for God (Pss. 18:46; 21:13; 46:11; 57:5, 11; 108:5). This is as bad as it gets—the place to which one looks for help is occupied by the enemy!

Verses 3-4 move beyond complaint to supplication. Three imperatives are supported by three reasons for God to act. The psalmist had asked four questions, and now he or she wants answers. The tone is still urgent. Death is mentioned as a real possibility if God fails to answer. The enemies are still pressing. Nothing yet has changed.

Verses 1-4 raise two traditional interpretative questions, which are related: (1) What is wrong with the psalmist? (2) Who is the enemy? Scholars have written thousands and thousands of pages trying to answer these two questions. As for the first, is the psalmist sick? Is the psalmist suffering from some terrible misfortune? Has the psalmist been falsely accused of a crime? How one approaches these questions then determines how one proceeds to identify the enemies. They may be false accusers, or they are persons who, on the basis of the psalmist's sickness or suffering, conclude that the psalmist must have committed some terrible sin and should be isolated from the community.[13] The fact of the matter is that we simply cannot conclusively answer these two questions. Scholars, who tend to like to pin things down, may find this frustrating. But what frustrates scholars is an advantage for faithful persons who pray the Psalms and look to them for instruction. As Miller puts it:

> The search for a readily identifiable situation as the context for understanding the laments may, however, be illusory or unnecessary. The language of these psalms with its stereotypical, generalizing, and figurative style is so open-ended that later readers, on the one hand, are stopped from peering behind them to one or more clearly definable sets of circumstances or settings in life, and on the other hand, are intentionally set free to adapt them to varying circumstances and settings.[14]

In other words, the really pertinent questions in reading Psalm 13 are these: What is wrong with us? Who and/or what are our enemies? From this perspective, we begin to see what the laments teach us about prayer and identity. Prayer is meant to be *honest!* Psalm 13 is bold, brash, even what many would consider blasphemous: "How long will you hide your face from me?" We are accustomed to prayers that are nice, polite, phrased in flowery language. To be sure, we may pray for the sick and suffering and dying, but the really raw edges of our lives and experience are often eliminated from conversations with God. They are reserved instead for conversations with the clinical psychologist or the family therapist or the marriage counselor or the social worker or perhaps even the lawyer or the judge. This may be fine, of course, but Psalm 13 and the other laments instruct us that God expects to hear our complaints, our troubles, our turmoil. Nothing is ruled out!

Prayer is not only the honest articulation of how "life isn't right" (vv. 1-2), but it is also supplication to God about the painful realities of life and death (vv. 3-4). The laments challenge us to locate our pain, the pain of others, the pain of the world, and to make all this the subject of our prayers. As Walter Brueggemann says, "How wondrous that these Psalms make it clear that precisely such dimensions of our life are the stuff of prayer."[15]

In teaching us about prayer, the laments also teach us about identity—about ourselves, the world, and God. Psalm 13 holds together these three realms of experience that we are inclined to separate—the psychological (the "I"), the sociological (the other/the enemy/the world), the theological (God).[16] The psalmist's inner experience is inextricably related to and inevitably described as an experience of God and the world. We learn the valuable lesson that our human experience is marvelously complex and ambiguous. While God's involvement in the world does not consist of God's pulling all the strings or manipulating all the causes that make things happen, God *is* involved. God is present in the depths; God is to be found where we live every day; God is with us. God is personally, intimately, concretely involved. Amid the complex, complicated, ambiguous, messy realities of our lives and the life of the world, God is present and active to fulfill ultimately God's purposes for human life and all creation. The transition from verse 4 to verses 5-6 will reinforce this message.

The laments' challenge to us to locate our pain and the pain of the world is particularly important in the kind of culture we live in. As M. Douglas Meeks points out, the growing realization that our resources are gradually becoming more scarce creates a nagging sense of insecurity even amid suffocating satiety:

> The conspiracy of scarcity, satiation, and security issues in a household without memory and hope. We are a society of amnesia. Our everyday modalities of life make us forgetful. It is increasingly difficult to remember not only our public history but also our personal stories. . . .
>
> Scarcity, satiation, and security not only produce amnesia, but also anesthesia. Drugs, alcohol, overconsumption, narcotics for overconsumption, passive absorption in television, and the compulsion to batten down the hatches all have the effect of making us insensitive to the suffering around us and too inert to remember what we have a right to hope for.[17]

In short, we have forgotten who we are, individually and corporately. We are easy prey for advertisers who regularly succeed in convincing us that our lives will be wonderful if we just drive the quietest car, drink the best-tasting soft drink, roll on the deodorant that will keep us cool under pressure, or vacation in those exotic places all over the world that take the VISA card instead of American Express. We are easy prey for politicians whose simplistic slogans about prosperity and progress regularly succeed in making us forget that we live in the most brutal and frightening era in human history—the century of Auschwitz, the killing fields, the nuclear bomb, Tiananmen Square, the depletion of the ozone layer, the proliferation of cancer and AIDS in the most medically sophisticated society of all time. We are easy prey for the media, whose second-by-second coverage of the recent Persian Gulf War managed not to sensitize us but rather to anesthetize us to the horrors of war. Even as I write, huge "victory celebrations" are taking place in Washington, D.C., and New York City, cheered on by millions of decent American citizens who either do not know or do not care that 170,000 Iraqi children will likely die in the next twelve months because our "smart bombs" devastated Iraq's infrastructure, leaving it without the ability to purify water and treat sewage.[18]

Lance Marrow, in a recent *Time* essay, is correct:

> It is touching in this era, and rather strange, that nature, even at its most destructive, has clean hands. Humankind does not. For centuries, nature's potential for evil, its overpowering menace, made it an enemy to be subdued. Today, at least in the developed world, nature is the vulnerable innocent. The human is the enemy.[19]

Strangely in this most brutal and frightening of eras, we have forgotten how violent and vulnerable we are, due perhaps to our vast scientific knowledge, our dazzling technology, our increasing life-spans, our abundance of possessions. We have forgotten who we are; it's an identity crisis of global proportions.

In his treatment of prayer in the Psalter, Mays points us to the potential power of the laments to teach us again who we are:

> In the long view, ultimately speaking, there is no technical or scientific solution to the reality of human finitude and sinfulness. To be human is to desire life and rightness, and because we cannot autonomously secure either, to be essentially needy.
> Could we use these prayers to learn that, admit that, learn from them to nurture a consciousness structured by an honest sense of our finitude and fallibility?[20]

Can we learn from Psalms 3, 13, 130, and the other laments that "the human is the enemy"? Can we be instructed to understand the difference between the "needs" created by clever advertisers and the way in which we are indeed "essentially needy"? Can we be moved to affirm with the psalmist, "Help belongs to the LORD" (Ps. 3:8)? Instructed by the Psalms and open to the grace of God, the answer may be yes.

Verses 5-6

The movement from the complaint of verses 1-2 to the supplication of verses 3-4 is logical and not unexpected; however, verses 5-6 are quite a surprise. What an abrupt about-face! Complaint and plea have given way to whole-hearted trust in God's *ḥesed* (see Pss. 130:7; 100:5; 117:2). The repetition of the word *heart* in verse 5 emphasizes the remarkable turn. "Sorrow in my *heart*" (v. 3) has been replaced by the affirmation "my *heart* shall *rejoice* in your salvation" (v. 5; "salvation" is the same Hebrew word translated as "help" in Psalm 3). Only one verse earlier, the foes *"rejoice* because I am shaken" (v. 4). The very last word of the psalm, "over me" (*ʿālāy*), provides a marked contrast to the final word of the complaint in verse 2. There, the enemy is "exalted *over me*" (my translation), but as the psalm ends, the affirmation is literally that God "has dealt out bounty *over me."* Suddenly, unexpectedly, dramatically, unequivocally, the "shaken" psalmist of verse 4 seems to have become a pillar of strength!

The remarkable transition between verse 4 and verse 5 poses the primary interpretative issue for the psalms of complaint or lament. How do we explain the abrupt change of mood? Should we envision a long wait between verse 4 and verse 5, during which the psalmist's situation has changed significantly for the better so that he or she can now rejoice instead of complain and plead?[21] Or should we imagine a Temple ritual or even a family setting in which a priest or representative of the synagogue delivered between verses 4 and 5 a now-missing salvation oracle, to which the suffering person responded with an affirmation of faith in anticipation of a future deliverance?[22]

In short, does Psalm 13:5-6 look back in gratitude or look forward in trust? Or, perhaps, is this to pose the issue wrongly? Is there another alternative? Mays, drawing upon Martin Luther, provides an interpretation of Psalm 13 that departs from the apparent *chronological* contradiction to arrive at a *theological* testimony:

> There is a powerful testimony to God in what seems a serious inconsistency in the prayer. It speaks to God in complaint *and* praise, speaks out of the experience of forsakeness *and* of grace, of abandonment *and* salvation. Interpreters have sought all kinds of ways to hold the two together to make sense of their juxtaposition. They speak of a movement of mood in which the psalmist wins his way by prayer from the darkness of despair to a joyous hope of ultimate deliverance. Or they reckon with a cultic procedure in which a response to the petition is given by a priest in the midst of the prayer to encourage the transition. But some knew better. Luther in his exposition of the Psalm calls the mood of the prayer the "state in which hope despairs, and yet despair hopes at the same time. . . . "
> There is a coherence which holds the apparently separate moments together. God is so much a god of blessing and salvation for the psalmist that he must speak of tribulation and terror as the absence of God. Yet God is so much the God of *ḥesed* [NRSV, "steadfast love"] for the psalmist that he can speak to God in the midst of tribulation and terror as the God of his salvation. This is the deep radical knowledge of faith which cannot separate God from any experience of life and perseveres

in construing all, including life's worst, in terms of relation to God. It is the expression of such a powerful experience of graciousness that it refuses to see the present apart from God and cannot imagine the future apart from his salvation. . . .

So in taking up the Psalm as our prayer, we are shown who we are when we pray. We are taught our true identity as mortals who stand on the earth and speak to a God who is ours but never owned. Agony and adoration hung together by a cry for life—this is the truth about us as people of faith. As the elect of God, we are not one but two—a duality fused and merged by the knowledge that our life depends on God. . . .

. . . The Psalm is not given us to use on the rare occasions when some trouble seems to make it appropriate. It is forever appropriate as long as life shall last. We do not begin at one end and come out at the other. The agony and the ecstasy belong together as the secret of our identity.[23]

By holding together the apparently separate moments or movements or moods, we learn both about God and ourselves. God has to do with all of life, and all of life has to do with God—even life's worst, even a cross. God is involved; God is with us.

As for us, we are simultaneously confronted and comforted—confronted again by our own finitude and fallibility and comforted by the good news of God's faithful love and grace. The agony and the ecstacy belong together. We are people both of the cross and of the resurrection—at one and the same time. Psalm 13 reminds us that there is no following Jesus without taking up our cross (Mark 8:34); and Psalm 13 also reminds us that anyone who loses his or her life for Jesus' "sake and the gospel's will save it" (Mark 8:35 RSV). Our identity ultimately is simple yet scandalous in a secular society; we are, as the apostle Paul put it, "children of God, and if children, then heirs, heirs of God and joint heirs with Christ—if, in fact, we suffer with him so that we may also be glorified with him" (Rom. 8:16-17).[24] Indeed, "The agony and the ecstacy belong together as the secret of our identity."

In Peter De Vries's novel *The Blood of the Lamb*, the narrator describes a strange scene from his youth that was spent assisting his father, who drove a garbage truck. One evening, his father backed the truck too close to the dump site; the truck turned upside down, leaving its two occupants in danger of being swallowed by the pit.

> Our truck lay in this position for only a few seconds, then it began to roll and tumble down the slope in the avalanche it had itself unloosed. The horror of this was followed instantly by a worse sight. The box on which my father stood was sucked away in the landslide—or perhaps I should say garbageslide—and he disappeared from view, singing the doxology.[25]

This unlikely episode provides an apt illustration of how the psalmists prayed and how we are taught to pray. In the pit, out of the depths, they and we raise our cries of complaint *and* our songs of praise. The agony and the ecstacy belong together.

PSALM 88: DARKNESS ALL DAY

Psalms 3, 13, and 130 are characteristic of the prayers of lament or complaint in that each exhibits (although in different ways) the movement beyond complaint and supplication to an expression of trust and/or praise.[26] Psalm 88 does not and is thus quite exceptional. As in the other laments, the cry or call arises "out of the depths." Three different Hebrew words for "cry" or "call" are used, as if to indicate that the psalmist has exhausted every approach. The urgency of the psalmist's plight is indicated by the range of vocabulary associated with death—Sheol (v. 3), Pit (vv. 4, 6), dead/death (vv. 5, 10, 15), grave (vv. 5, 11), dark/darkness (vv. 5, 12, 18), deep (v. 6), shades (v. 10), Abaddon (v. 11), land of forgetfulness (v. 12). Noteworthy too are the chronological references—"at night" (v. 1); "every day" (or "all day," v. 9); "in the morning" (v. 13)—each associated with one of the psalmist's cries. Every possible approach, at every possible moment, has been tried, and the result is "darkness," literally the final word of the psalm. The word *darkness* (*ḥōšek*, v. 12) or *dark place(s)* (*maḥšāk*, vv. 6, 18) occurrs in each section of the psalm; darkness pervades the psalm and the psalmist's experience. It is darkness all day long.[27]

The theological problems and possibilities of Psalm 88 are posed sharply by verses 8 and 18. God has caused the psalmist's isolation (note the repetition of the *hiphil* of *rhq* in verses 8 and 18—literally, "You have caused to be far . . . ")! God is the problem (see also vv. 14, 16-17), but God is also the solution. Even life's worst has to do with God, and so the cry goes up out of the depths.

Two statements by Brueggemann define the theological issue: "Psalm 88 is an embarrassment to conventional faith." "Psalm 88 shows us what the cross is about: *faithfulness* in scenes of complete *abandonment*."[28]

These statements may sound contradictory, until we realize that there was and is nothing "conventional" about the cross, "a stumbling block to Jews and foolishness to Gentiles" (1 Cor. 1:23). To be sure, Psalm 88 is not a prediction of Jesus' suffering, but it serves to articulate the same experience Jesus would later live out. Facing the cross, Jesus' soul was "full of troubles" (v. 3; see Mark 14:33-34). He was shunned even by those closest to him (vv. 8, 18; see Mark 14:50). His one companion was darkness (v. 18; see Mark 15:33). And like the psalmist, who out of the darkness still appeals to God, Jesus was faithful. In the midst of abandonment, his cry is still, "My God, my God" (Mark 15:34).[29] In short, Psalm 88 not only provides us with a way to articulate in the most extreme way that "life isn't right," but it also offers testimony to the extremes that God is willing to go to demonstrate faithful love for humanity. As the psalmist in Psalm 88 suffered, so God's Son suffered life's worst for us. That is what the cross is about. God loves us *that* much! And there is nothing "conventional" about that kind of love—it is neither fair nor just. Sheer grace is always a scandal.

The exceptional, extreme character of Psalm 88 makes it a valuable theological and pastoral resource at all times, but perhaps especially when we have trouble perceiving any ecstacy at all accompanying our agony. When Presbyterian missionary Benjamin Weir was being held hostage in Lebanon, the Presbyterian Church distributed resources to be used in prayer services for him and other hostages. One of the Scripture passages suggested by Carol Weir, Ben's wife, was Psalm 88. In his novel _Sophie's Choice,_ William Styron also illustrates the value of Psalm 88 as a theological resource. The main character, Stingo, is returning to New York City to confront a terrible tragedy. Stingo and an African-American woman sitting beside him on the train begin to read the Bible, a "prescription for my torment," as Stingo puts it.

> "Psalm Eighty-eight," I would suggest. To which she would reply, "Dat is some fine psalm." We read aloud through Wilmington, Chester, and past Trenton, turning from time to time to Ecclesiastes and Isaiah. After a while we tried the Sermon on the Mount, but somehow it didn't work for me; the grand old Hebrew woe seemed more cathartic, so we went back to Job.[30]

To read Psalm 88 may well be "cathartic," but it is more. It is also faithful and instructive. To read Psalm 88 reminds us that even when we stand in utter darkness, we do not stand alone. We stand with the psalmist of old. We stand with Christ on the cross. To cry into the darkness "O LORD, my God" (Ps. 88:1) is an act of solidarity with the communion of saints and an act of faith and hope—indeed, an affirmation of the hope of the resurrection.

CHAPTER 6

PRAYER AND IDENTITY: FOR I KNOW MY TRANSGRESSIONS

Everything we learned about prayer and identity in chapter 5 applies as well to the psalms we shall examine in this chapter. Like Psalm 130, Psalms 51 and 32 are cases in which the "depths" involve the psalmist's own sinfulness. Psalms 32, 51, and 130 are among a group of seven Penitential Psalms, which personalize and sharpen the focus of the Psalms' instruction about human finitude and sinfulness.[1] As suggested in chapter 5 on the basis of Psalm 130, the Penitential Psalms end up being much more than prayers of confession; they become powerful proclamations of the good news. Of particular interest in Psalms 32 and 51 is the explicitly instructional intent of the psalmist (32:8-9; 51:13). One could call it an evangelistic thrust, and it is not surprising that the apostle Paul drew upon several of the Penitential Psalms to proclaim the good news of the justification of sinful humanity by God's grace revealed in Jesus Christ.

PSALM 51[2]

The superscription of Psalm 51 is the first clue that the psalm is ultimately about the justification of a sinner by grace. The superscription invites the reader to hear Psalm 51 in the con-

text of the story of David's taking of Bathsheba and subsequent murder of her husband Uriah (2 Samuel 11). If ever
anyone deserved to be punished, it was David, whose after-
noon stroll on the roof led him eventually to break fully half of
the Ten Commandments (David killed, committed adultery,
stole, bore false witness, and coveted). Remarkably, David is
forgiven (2 Sam. 12:13); he lives; he remains king. What is
determinative in the story is not David's character but rather
God's character. God's *hesed*, "steadfast love," prevails (see 2
Sam. 7:15).[3]

It is precisely to *God's* character that the psalmist appeals in
Psalm 51:1:

> Have mercy on me [*hannēnî*], O God,
>   according to your steadfast love [*hesed*];
>   according to your abundant mercy [*rahămîm*]
>   blot out my transgressions.

Before any mention of the vocabulary of sin, which dominates
verses 1-5, the psalmist appeals to God's character, using
three key words from God's self-revelation in Exodus 34:6:
"merciful" (*rahûm*), "gracious" (*hannûn*), and "steadfast love"
(*hesed*). As in 2 Samuel 11–12, so in Exodus 32–34, it is God's
character and not human sinfulness that is determinative and
that keeps the story going. Both Israel and David are justified,
made right with God, by *God's* grace. So it is with the psalmist, in Psalm 51, who quite rightly admits that God is "justified [*tisdaq*] in your sentence" (v. 4), but later affirms also that
"my tongue will sing aloud of your deliverance" [*sidqāteka*,
literally, "your justification"/"your setting things right"] (v.
14). The psalmist has been or anticipates being justified by
God's grace.

After appealing to God's character, the psalmist turns to his
own sinfulness. The vocabulary of sin pervades verses 1-5—
"transgression" (vv. 1, 3), "iniquity" (vv. 2, 5, NRSV "guilty" in
v. 5), "sin" (vv. 2-5,), "evil" (v. 4). In verses 2-5, the most
general Hebrew word for "sin" (*ht'*) is paired with a nearly
synonymous but more specialized word; "iniquity" (vv. 2, 5)
involves the personal guilt or culpability of the sinner; "trans-

gression" (v. 3) suggests willful rebellion; "evil" (v. 4) conveys the injurious effects of sinful behavior. The effect of the repetition is to drive home the point. Sin and its consequences are pervasive. The climatic verse 5 has traditionally been cited in discussions of "original sin," and rightfully so. While it is not intended to suggest that sin is transmitted biologically, verse 5 does suggest that human fallibility is inevitable. In each human life, in the human situation, sin is pervasive; we are born into it. The literary device of repetition reinforces the psalmist's theological point—sin pervades the human situation.

The narrative contexts suggested above make the same point. In Exodus 32–34, the people whom God delivered prove immediately to be disobedient. God's story with God's people will not continue unless God is merciful, gracious, and abundant in steadfast love (Exod. 34:6), precisely because the people's behavior involves "iniquity and transgression and sin" (Exod. 34:7)—the same three words that dominate Psalm 51:1-5. When God initiates a monarchy at the people's request, the kings prove immediately to be disobedient. Saul is rejected in favor of David, whose behavior is "evil" (2 Sam. 12:9) and who frankly admits, "I have sinned against the LORD" (2 Sam. 12:13). God's willingness to forgive, God's steadfast love, keep the story going.

Israel's story, David's story, and the psalmist's story testify to the same reality—sin pervades the human situation. Comedian A. Whitney Brown states the reality well as he reflects on what he calls "The Big Picture":

> There's a lot we should be able to learn from history. And yet history proves that we never do. In fact, the main lesson of history is that we never learn the lessons of history. This makes us look so stupid that few people care to read it. They'd rather not be reminded. Any good history book is mainly just a long list of mistakes, complete with names and dates. It's very embarrassing.[4]

Israel's story is indeed "a long list of mistakes"; Exodus 32–34 proves to be paradigmatic of the whole history of Israel.[5] David's story and the history of the subsequent monarchy are indeed "very embarrassing." So is the psalmist's story in Psalm 51. So is the behavior of the disciples in the Gospels. So is the situation of the early church revealed in the letters of Paul. So is the history of the Christian church throughout the centuries. So is the denominational and congregational life of the contemporary church. So are the details of our life stories, if we are honest enough to admit it. In short, Psalm 51 is about *us!* It is about who we are as individuals, families, churches—sin pervades our lives. It's very embarrassing.

Our only help, our only hope, is to do what the psalmist did: abandon the attempt to justify ourselves and appeal instead to the character of God. The appeal of verses 1-2 is renewed in verse 6, where the verb *teach* (*hiphil* of *yd* , literally "cause me to know") initiates a series of imperatives that extends through verse 15, with the interesting exception of verse 13 (see below). Verses 16-17 contain no further imperatives, but they seem to close out the section that begins in verse 6. In particular, the repetition of "spirit" and "heart" link verse 17 to verses 10-12. Much of the imagery of the appeal in verses 1-2, 6-17 alludes to cultic rituals, the exact nature of which are unknown to us—"wash" (vv. 2, 7); "cleanse"/"clean" (vv. 2, 7, 10); "blot out" (vv. 1, 9). The real point, however, is that by God's action, the psalmist has been or will be transformed.

This point is particularly evident in verses 10-13, which lie at the heart of the larger section, verses 6-17. The verb *br'*, "create," is used in the Old Testament only of God's activity. It is particularly prominent in the opening chapters of Genesis (1:1, 21, 27; 2:3, 4, etc.) and in Isaiah 40–55, where God's creative activity involves the doing of a "new thing" (Isa. 43:15-19; 48:6-7; see also 41:20; 45:7-8). The verb can also be used to describe birth (Ezek. 28:13-15; Ps. 102:18). The psalmist affirms, in effect, that he has been reborn. It is significant that the verb *br'* also occurs in the context of God's self-revelation in Exodus 34:6-7. Immediately following the self-revelation, Moses appeals to God that the "LORD go with us" and "pardon our iniquity and our sin" (Exod. 34:9). God responds by making a covenant (which in the final form of the book of

Exodus must be understood already as a *new* covenant; see the covenant ceremony described in 24:1-8) and by promising to "perform marvels, such as have not been performed [*nibreû;* literally, "been created"] in all the earth or in any nation" (34:10). In short, it is God's fundamental character to restore, rehabilitate, recreate sinners. Israel's life depended on it; David's life and dynasty depended on it; the psalmist's life depended on it; our life depends on it.

The apostle Paul knew this fundamental reality about God. He saw it most clearly revealed in Jesus Christ; and he proclaimed it to the Corinthians in terms reminiscent of Psalm 51:10-13:

> So if anyone is in Christ, there is a new creation; everything old has passed away; see, everything has become new! All this is from God, who reconciled us to himself through Christ, and has given us the ministry of reconciliation; that is, in Christ God was reconciling the world to himself, not counting their trespasses against them, and entrusting the message of reconciliation to us. So we are ambassadors for Christ, since God is making his appeal through us; we entreat you on behalf of Christ, be reconciled to God. (2 Cor. 5:17-20)

Saul, the former murderer, has become Paul, ambassador for Christ. By God's grace, everything has become new!

The repetition of the word *spirit* (*rûaḥ*) in Psalm 51:10-12 reinforces the good news. This word is also suggestive of God's creative activity. In Genesis 1:2, it is God's *rûaḥ* that moves over the deep; God's *rûaḥ* is responsible for all life and its sustenance (see Job 34:14-15). For the psalmist to receive a new spirit (v. 10), to live in the presence of God's spirit (v. 11), and to be sustained by God's spirit (v. 12) means nothing short of new life. Again, Psalm 51 anticipates the experience of the apostle Paul, who describes his transformation by saying, "It is no longer I who live, but it is Christ who lives in me" (Gal. 2:20). For Paul as for the psalmist, there is a new creation. Everything has become new!

This new creation accounts for Paul's amazing movement from persecution of the church to apostle to the Gentiles.

Similarly, it is this new creation that accounts for the psalm-ist's remarkable promise in verse 13:

> Then I will teach transgressors your ways,
> and sinners will return to you.

The vocabulary that dominates verses 1-5 recurs in verse 13, but with a twist. The chief among transgressors and sinners is now the *teacher* of transgressors and sinners. The reconciled bears the message of reconciliation. The one who appealed to God becomes the ambassador through whom God's appeal is made. There is a new creation. Everything has become new!

It is the psalmist's promise to teach transgressors and sin-ners, which I mentioned earlier as the evangelistic thrust of Psalm 51. The recipient of new life becomes an evangelist, a witness, a teacher. In the Gospel of John, as the risen Christ commissions his disciples, he breathes on them and says, "Re-ceive the Holy Spirit" (20:22). In a similar scene at the end of the Gospel of Matthew, the risen Christ sends his disciples to all nations, and their mission specifically involves "teaching them to obey everything I have commanded you" (28:20). Jesus' newly commissioned disciples are the same persons who only recently had "deserted him and fled" (26:56). New life means new work to do.[6] There is a new creation. Every-thing has become new!

This understanding of verse 13 affects the interpretation of verse 14 as well. The opening line of verse 14 is richly ambigu-ous: "Deliver me from bloodguiltiness" (RSV) or "Deliver me from bloodshed" (NRSV). The Hebrew word in question (*dāmîm*) can mean the guilt incurred from shedding blood, as the RSV suggests. This meaning would be suitable for one who has presented oneself as chief among sinners, especially when Psalm 51 is heard in the narrative context of David's murder of Uriah. In this case, verse 14 continues the appeal for forgiveness in verses 1-2 and 6-12. However, the Hebrew word can also mean "bloodshed" or "violence," as the NRSV sug-gests. In the light of verse 13, this meaning is particularly appropriate. The psalmist's appeal now is not for forgiveness but rather for protection as he fulfills his mission. After all, the psalmist, in the light of the way he described himself in verses 1-5, would not very readily be perceived as a credible teacher of sinners and transgressors. Again, we are reminded of the apostle Paul. After his remarkable transformation, Paul was not readily received by the Christian community. Ananias hesitated to associate with Paul, because he had heard "how much *evil* [Paul] has done to your saints in Jerusalem" (Acts 9:13). The disciples in Jerusalem were all afraid of Paul (Acts 9:26). As for Paul himself, his life was in danger, as it would be constantly throughout his ministry (Acts 9:29). Paul would always need to pray, as the psalmist prayed in verse 14, "Deliver me from bloodshed." Sheer grace is always a scandal. In every place and time, those who faithfully witness to the grace of God will always need to pray: "Deliver me from bloodshed."[7]

Despite opposition or anticipated opposition, the psalmist is committed to making a public witness. An inward transformation is not sufficient. The "clean heart" and "new . . . spirit" will be accompanied by outwardly visible and audible proclamation. God's "new thing" must be declared. Every organ of speech will participate—"my tongue," "my lips," "my mouth" (vv. 14-15). This outpouring of praise is apparently intended to replace what may have customarily been offered as a public witness—namely, a ritual sacrifice (v. 16). The psalmist's sacrifice is "a broken spirit; a broken and contrite heart" (v. 17). The Hebrew root of the word translated "contrite" in verse 17 is the same as for the word translated "crushed" in verse 8 (RSV "broken"). The psalmist's "broken" bones have been replaced by a "broken" heart—further evidence of the psalmist's transformation. If pride is the fundamental sin that inevitably leads to idolatry, then the transformed psalmist now evidences a humility that inevitably leads to praise. He is offering to God his whole self. The psalmist has much to proclaim, but it is not about himself. It is about God: "My mouth will declare your praise" (v. 15). The psalmist's public witness is directed at precisely the same thing as was his urgent appeal—at the character of God. To cite the apostle Paul again, "Let the one who boasts, boast in the Lord" (1 Cor. 1:31; see 2 Cor. 11:30; 12:5-10).

The several parallels we have drawn between Psalm 51 and the letters and ministry of Paul should not be surprising. Psalm 51 is essentially a proclamation of the good news of the justification of sinners by God's grace, the good news Paul saw revealed most clearly in the crucifixion and resurrection of Jesus. Paul's fullest exposition of this good news is his letter to the Romans. Following the exposition in Romans 1–11, Paul lays out the implications for response in 12:1-2. His instruction is reminiscent of the point at which the psalmist arrives in 51:17 and the direction he took to get there:

> I appeal to you therefore, brothers and sisters, by the mercies of God, to present your bodies as a living sacrifice, holy and acceptable to God, which is your spiritual worship. Do not be conformed to this world, but be transformed by the renewing of your minds, so that you may discern what is the will of God— what is good and acceptable and perfect. (Rom. 12:1-2)

Without ever having heard it, the psalmist followed Paul's advice. By the mercies of God (51:1), he presented his whole self as a living sacrifice (51:17). The transformed psalmist begins to participate with God in transforming the world. There is a new creation. Everything is made new!

The final two verses of Psalm 51 seem to be a later addition to clarify the perspective on sacrifice in verses 16-17.[8] The effect of the final form of Psalm 51 is to give the intensely personal testimony of verses 1-17 a corporate dimension. The justification of the individual sinner does not obviate the need for participation in the worship of the community but rather enables proper participation. "Right sacrifices" will be offered by those who have first offered their whole selves to God. By the mercies of God, even the traditional rituals, the same old order of worship, will be transformed. Indeed, everything is made new!

PSALM 32[9]

As in Psalm 51, the vocabulary of sin dominates the first five verses of Psalm 32. The same three key words recur here—*transgression* (vv. 1, 5), *sin* (vv. 1, 5), *iniquity/guilt* (vv. 2, 5, 5). Sin is pervasive, but what the psalmist celebrates is the forgiveness of sin. Those who do not "hide" their iniquity will be the ones "whose sin is covered" ("hide" in v. 5 and "covered" in v. 1 are from the same Hebrew root, *ksh*). In terms of the literary structure of Psalm 32, God's forgiveness surrounds, emcompasses sin (vv. 1*a*, 5*c*; the Hebrew root translated "forgiven/forgave" is *nś*). The personal pronoun in verse 5*c* is emphatic, "*you* forgave the guilt of my sin." Furthermore, verse 5*c* is the turning point of the psalm. After this proclamation of forgiveness, things are different. This change is marked literarily by the fact that none of the words for sin occurs again. Everything has been made new!

From the first five verses, it is clear that the psalmist's confession of sin has been a cathartic, healing experience. But from the subsequent verses, it is just as clear that the psalmist's attention is focused not upon himself or herself. Rather, the psalmist immediately directs attention to others and to God: "Therefore, let all who are faithful offer prayer to you" (v. 6). The Hebrew for "faithful" is *ḥāsîd*, anticipating the occurrence of the related *ḥesed*, "steadfast love," in verse 10. The "faithful" derive their identity not from their own accomplishments but from *God's* faithfulness in forgiving them and renewing them. *God's* character is determinative. Prayer is a way of life for those who know that their own accomplishments, capabilities, and intentions are always inadequate.

Prayer is directed "to you"—God. The three affirmations in verse 7 focus attention directly on God, beginning with the pronoun *You*, which recalls the emphatic pronoun that began the final line of verse 5. In each of the three affirmations in verse 7, God is the actor and the psalmist is the object of God's action. Again, God's character and God's activity are determinative. As Robert Jenson suggests, "The psalmist's own stance is that of *witness*, to his experience and to the grace of God."[10]

The vocabulary of the third affirmation in verse 7 anticipates verses 10 and 11 and intensifies the focus on God's character and activity: "You surround me with glad cries of deliverance." "Surround" recurs in verse 10 where God's ḥesed "surrounds those who trust in the LORD." The psalm ends as the upright are invited to "shout for joy," repeating the root of the "glad cries" of verse 7. This invitation is possible only because God has already surrounded the psalmist with "glad cries." God's prior action is determinative. God's grace is fundamental.

Interpreters disagree as to the speaker in verse 8. Is it God instructing the psalmist? Or is it the psalmist instructing others? Given the psalmist's stance as witness to God's grace in verse 7, it is most likely that verse 8 is an extension of the psalmist's witness. As in Psalm 51:13, the forgiven sinner, renewed by God's grace, teaches others God's way. The psalmist's educational mission is not presumptuous. The witness is not to the psalmist's own faithfulness and rightness but to *God's* faithfulness and God's ability to set things and persons right. The "way you should go" (v. 8) is not a blueprint for moral perfection but rather consists of the psalmist's own example of humbly confessing one's sinfulness and yielding one's life to God (v. 10).

Psalm 32 is an important check against self-righteousness and legalism. It is perhaps not coincidental and certainly not insignificant that much of the vocabulary of Psalm 32 recalls Psalm 1—"Happy" (vv. 1-2; see Ps. 1:1); "sin" (vv. 1, 5; see "sinners" in Ps. 1:1, 5); "day and night" (v. 4; see Ps. 1:2); "teach" (v. 8; the root is the same as the word for *torah*/"law"/"instruction" in Ps. 1:2); "way" (v. 8; see Ps. 1:1, 6); "wicked" (v. 10; see Ps. 1:1, 4-6); and "righteous" (v. 11; see Ps. 1:5-6). Psalm 32 reinforces the understanding of righteousness which we reached on the basis of Psalm 1. To be righteous is not to manage somehow to obey all the rules, to be sinless, to be morally perfect. In fact, as Psalms 32 and 51 suggest, the life of the righteous is pervaded by sin and its consequences. To be righteous is to be forgiven, to be open to God's instruction, to live in dependence upon God rather than self. In short, to be righteous is to be a witness to God's grace.

One of the greatest witnesses to God's grace, the apostle Paul, knew well Psalm 32 and cited verses 1-2 in his own teaching in Romans 4:6-8. Paul did not invent the notion of justification by grace. He found it in the story of Abraham, and he found it in psalms, such as Psalms 32 and 51. Another of the greatest witnesses to God's grace, St. Augustine, had the words of Psalm 32 inscribed above his bed so that they would be the first thing he saw every morning upon awakening.[11]

It is not coincidental that Psalm 33 takes up the invitation to praise that concludes Psalm 32. The "righteous" and "upright" (Ps. 33:1; see Ps. 32:11) are invited to sing a "new song" (Ps. 33:3), which is the appropriate response to God's renewing grace. It is as if the whole congregation of God's people confirms the witness to God's grace offered by the "I" in Psalm 32. Psalm 33 ends in the same way Psalm 32 does, except the testimony is now in the plural. The whole congregation is "glad" (32:11; 33:21) in affirming its "trust" (32:10; 33:21) in God's *ḥesed* (32:10; 33:18, 22). The psalmist's instruction (32:8) has been heard and heeded. Psalm 33 recognizes the inadequacy of even the greatest human accomplishments (vv. 16-17). Psalm 33 illustrates, therefore, what always "befits" (33:1) finite and fallible human beings—praise for God's *ḥesed* (vv. 4-5) and prayer for God's *ḥesed* (v. 22). The good news is that *God's* character and activity are determinative.

CHAPTER 7

PRAYER AND ACTIVITY: VENGEANCE, CATHARSIS, AND COMPASSION

There is a prominent feature of the prayers in the Psalter that we have yet to address and that many persons find very troubling—namely, the psalmist's expression of the desire for vengeance upon his or her enemies. While these prayers are often viewed as morally inferior and "un-Christian," they have profound insights to offer about God, about ourselves, and about the basis of both God's activity and human activity that seeks to conform to God's will. We shall begin with the worst-case scenario, Psalm 109. It will raise the basic issues that will be explored further with the help of Psalms 137 and 82.

PSALM 109

In many ways, Psalm 109 conforms to the structure, movement, and content of the laments discussed in chapter 5. The element of lament/complaint (vv. 2-5, 22-25) is accompanied by supplication (vv. 1*a*, 20-21, 26-29), and the psalm ends with praise and an affirmation of trust (vv. 30-31). In between, however, in verses 6-19, there is what Brueggemann has aptly called a "song of hate."[1] After verses 4-5 describe how the psalmist has loved the enemy to no avail, verse 6 suggests that the psalmist has finally suffered all that he or she can endure. Some redress must be sought, and the psalmist's request for redress begins in verse 6. (The NRSV has inserted, "They say" before v. 6, thus attributing the "song of hate" to the enemies; I am following the RSV, which accurately translates the Hebrew).[2] The request begins moderately enough: as the psalmist has been the target of wicked behavior (v. 2), so let the enemy now experience the same. Having been accused (v. 4), the psalmist now asks for an accuser against the enemy. The Hebrew word for "accuser" is *śāṭān*, and it should be understood as something like a "special prosecutor." The behavior of the enemy must be investigated, and verse 6 requests the initiation of what seems like fair and due process.

Verse 7, however, leaves due process behind. An investigation or trial is really not necessary. The verdict can already be pronounced: Guilty! And so can the sentence (vv. 8-19). In announcing the sentence the enemy deserves, the psalmist's desire for revenge leaves no base untouched. Not only is the enemy himself the target (vv. 8, 11-12, 12-19), but also are his wife (v. 9), his children (vv. 6-10, 12), his posterity, any future remembrance of his name (v. 13), and even his ancestors (v. 14). The hyperbole would be comic were it not for the utter seriousness of the psalmist's request—let the enemy be completely annihilated!

In a real sense, the psalmist's desire for vengeance is simply the expression of a notion that most Americans cherish and that our legal system attempts to implement—namely, that the punishment should fit the crime. The enemy deserves no "kindness" (v. 12), because he showed no "kindness" (v. 16). The enemy deserves to be impoverished (vv. 8-11), because he mistreated the poor and needy (v. 16). The enemy deserves to be cursed, because he cursed others (vv. 17-19, 28-29). In short, the enemy deserves to die (v. 8), because he pursued others to their deaths (vv. 16, 31).

In a society where most people, including most Christians, favor the death penalty, the desire for vengeance expressed in Psalm 109 really should not present us with much of a problem. And yet, my experience in talking about Psalm 109 with groups in churches reveals that people are quick to conclude that Psalm 109 is "un-Christian." Jesus said to love one's enemies, turn the other cheek, go the second mile. The psalmist does not measure up.

The disparity between the standard we affirm and systematically implement and the standard to which we hold the psalmist is the initial clue to what we Christians can learn from Psalm 109. If we are honest, we must conclude that Psalm 109 teaches us about ourselves. *We* are vengeful creatures. I recently read a book to my five-year-old daughter, and her response illustrates the point. The book uses bears as characters but intends to address children's concerns. In this case, one bear cub had mistreated and excluded another bear cub, whose feelings were hurt. Eventually, the perpetrator recognized her misdeeds and changed her ways. The book ends as the offending cub concludes that "I've learned *my* lesson."[3] My daughter, however, was not content to let the book end that way. She wanted to continue the story to include an episode where the perpetrator of exclusion would suffer the exclusion she had inflicted upon another. *We* are vengeful creatures! As Brueggemann concludes:

> The real theological problem, I submit, is not that vengeance is *there* in the Psalms, but that it is *here* in our midst. And that it is there and here only reflects how attuned the Psalter is to what goes on among us. Thus, we may begin with a recognition of the acute correspondence between what is *written there* and what is *practiced here*. The Psalms do "tell it like it is" with us.[4]

Psalm 109 not only tells it like it is with us, but it also tells us how it is with the world. The psalmist had been victimized; and when persons become victims, they are bound to react with rage. The recent riots in Los Angeles, in the wake of the Rodney King verdict, are ample illustration. As C. S. Lewis says about Psalm 109, it shows "the natural result of injuring a human being."[5] When persons are treated unjustly, we can expect them to lash out; we can expect them to express vehemently the desire for an end to the violence that has made them a victim.

Such expression of hurt and rage is not only to be expected, it is also to be accepted as a sign of health. Psalm 109 thus teaches us a basic principle of pastoral care: Anger is the legitimate response to victimization, and appropriate anger must be expressed. Such catharsis is healing. What Psalm 109 represents, however, is not merely a therapeutic movement. This is *theological* catharsis. The anger is expressed, but it is expressed in prayer to God and is thereby submitted to God. While it is not explicit, we may assume that the psalmist's submission of his or her anger to God in prayer was sufficient. This angry, honest prayer obviates the need for the psalmist to take actual revenge on the enemy. In short, it seems that the psalmist honors God's affirmation in Deuteronomy 32:35, "Vengeance is mine." This vehement, violent-sounding prayer is, in fact, an act of non-violence.[6]

In the final analysis then, Psalm 109 teaches us not only about ourselves and the world but also about God. It suggests that evil must be confronted, opposed, hated because God hates evil. The psalmist's desire for vengeance against the enemy sounds more acceptable perhaps when we state it a bit differently—"thy will be done." The psalmist opposes the enemy, because the enemy opposes God and God's purposes. God wills not victimization of persons but compassion for persons. The key word in Psalm 109 is *hesed*; its four-fold repetition (vv. 12, 16, 21, 26) highlights the theological message of the psalm. The basic indictment against the enemy is found in verse 16: "For he did not remember to show kindness [*hesed*],/ but pursued the poor and needy/ and the broken-hearted to their death."

In short, the enemy has failed to embody God's fundamental character—*hesed*. Thus the enemy's actions lead to death instead of life. Quite logically or theologically, the psalmist grounds his appeal precisely in the fundamental character of God. The emphatic "But *you*" of verse 21 sharpens the contrast between the enemy and God:

> But you, O LORD my Lord,
> act on my behalf for your name's sake;

> because your steadfast love [*ḥesed*] is
> good, deliver me.

God's "name's sake," God's fundamental identity, God's essential character, involves *ḥesed*. Verse 26 reinforces this message:

> Help me, O LORD my God!
> Save me according to your
> steadfast love [*ḥesed*].

Psalm 109 is an eloquent affirmation of God's compassion for the poor and needy, and this affirmation is the basis of the psalmist's appeal. The psalmist, who is poor and needy (v. 22; see v. 16), entrusts himself to God with the assurance that God "stands at the right hand of the needy" (v. 31). The language of verse 31 recalls two earlier verses—6 and 16. God stands in solidarity with those whom the enemy failed to remember compassionately (v. 16). The affirmation also recalls the psalmist's plea that "an accuser stand on his [the enemy's] right" (v. 6).[7] God's *ḥesed* means judgment upon the wicked for the sake of the poor and needy. Psalm 109 thus teaches us who God is and what God would have us do. God's fundamental character is to stand with and for the poor and needy. To be instructed by Psalm 109 is to take our stand with God and with the poor and needy.

To be sure, there is nothing morally inferior or "un-Christian" about this psalm as instruction. But what about Psalm 109 as a prayer? Can it be a Christian prayer? Can it be our prayer? In discussions of Psalm 109 in church groups, people have frequently told me that they have never been *that* angry. I believe them. Most persons who read this book have never been so completely victimized as the psalmist of Psalm 109. But if this means that Psalm 109 cannot be our prayer for ourselves, can it then be our prayer for others? In speaking of the psalmic prayers, Mays suggests this possibility in a moving and compelling way:

Could the use of these prayers remind us and bind us to all those in the world-wide Church who are suffering in faith and for faith? All may be well in our place. There may be no trouble for the present that corresponds to the tribulations described in the Psalms, but do we need to do more than call the roll of such places as El Salvador, South Africa, and China to remember that there are sisters and brothers whose trials could be given voice in our recitation of the Psalms? The old Church believed that it was all the martyrs who prayed in their praying the psalmic prayers.

Would it be possible to say them for the sake of and in the name of fellow Christians known to us? We do make intercessions for them, but perhaps these Psalms can help us do more than simply, prayerfully wish grace and help for them, help us to find words to represent their hurt, alienation, failure and discouragement. . . .

The apostle said that "If one member suffers, all suffer together" (1 Cor. 12:26), and he also said "Bear one another's burdens" (Gal. 6:2). Can these prayers become a way of doing that?[8]

Yes, they can. Psalm 109 teaches us and calls us to care for other persons, to bear one another's burdens, to stand in solidarity and in suffering with the poor and needy, because God "stands at the right hand of the needy,/ to save them from those who would condemn them to death" (v. 31).

PSALM 137

Psalm 137 raises the same issues and teaches the same lessons as Psalm 109, but with a different nuance that has made it more acceptable. Unlike Psalm 109, which is virtually never read or sung in Christian worship services, Psalm 137 is used frequently, albeit with the omission of the final verse (v. 9). Of course, it is this offensive-sounding final verse that makes Psalm 137 so much like Psalm 109. It expresses the desire for an oppressor to be punished in proportion to the crime committed. When verse 9 is read in conjunction with verse 8, the point is even clearer: "Happy shall they be who pay you back *what you have done to us!*" The Babylonian conquest of Judah in

587 B.C. certainly involved the death of many Judeans, including children. The psalmist suggests simply that the punishment of the Babylonians fit their crime. In this respect, Psalm 137 is like 109.

What is different about Psalm 137 and what has made it more acceptable is that it begins not with an expression of rage and desire for revenge, but rather with an expression of grief. The exiles weep (v. 1); they are unable to make music and sing (vv. 2-4). Grief is a more acceptable emotion than rage and the desire for revenge, which accompanies anger. But what Psalm 137 teaches is that grief and anger are inseparable, and it does so in an artistic way. The structure and vocabulary of the poem make the point.

Verses 1-4 express the exiles' grief. Verses 7-9 express the exiles' rage and desire for revenge. In between, at the literary and conceptual heart of the poem, verses 5-6 focus the hearer's attention on the crucial activity of remembering. The chiastic structure (*abba* pattern) of the lines provides further emphasis:

> a   If I *forget you*, O Jerusalem,
> b   let my *right hand* wither!
> b[1] Let my *tongue* cling to the roof of my mouth,
> a[1] if I do not *remember you*, . . .

As it is, "there" (vv. 1, 3) in Babylon, it is impossible to make music and sing. The other place, Jerusalem, is personified as "you" (vv. 5-6); and if this "you" is not remembered, music and song will be impossible *forever*. The right hand will be withered and the tongue paralyzed. In short, memory of Jerusalem, God's place, is what sustains life and hope in the midst of debilitating despair (vv. 1-4) and death's devastation (vv. 7-9).

It is not surprising that the central concept of remembering links verses 5-6 to verses 1-4, where the exiles remember Jerusalem (v. 1), and to verses 7-9, where the Lord is called upon to remember Jerusalem's fall (v. 7). The importance of memory is pervasive, literarily and conceptually. In Psalm 137, remembering means faithfulness to God's place and to God's ongo-

ing purposes. Remembering Jerusalem is an act of resistance—
"in a foreign land" (v. 4), God's people could not sing but they
could remember. Indeed, they had to remember!

The structure of Psalm 137 teaches us that the crucial act of
remembering is energized by the strong and inseparable emotions of grief and anger. In situations of victimization, both
grief and anger are not only inevitable, but also acceptable and
indeed necessary. In the case of Psalm 137, grief and anger
sustain the remembrance that makes faith, hope, and life possible "in a foreign land." In the face of monstrous evil, the
worst possible response is to feel *nothing*. What *must* be felt is
grief, rage, outrage. In their absence, evil becomes an acceptable commonplace. To forget is to submit to evil, to wither and
die; to remember is to resist, be faithful, and live again. In the
twentieth century, Psalm 137 cannot help reminding us of the
Holocaust, the monstrous victimization of the Jewish people
during World War II. Holocaust survivor Elie Wiesel has dedicated his life to making sure the world remembers what happened. Wiesel says frequently that he can tolerate the memory
of silence but not the silence of memory. In short, the Holocaust can be remembered in *unutterable* horror—silence. But it
must be remembered. To remember is painful; grief is always
painful. To remember is unsettling; anger always unsettles.
But to remember is also to resist the same thing happening
again. To remember is to live and to be faithful to God's
purpose of life for all people.

Given the mention of "little ones" in Psalm 137:9, it is especially revealing to consider Wiesel's special concern for children. It is perhaps a clue to the ultimate direction and
significance of remembering in Psalm 137—namely, grief and
rage eventually energize a memory that takes the form of
compassion. As in Psalm 109, the psalmist in Psalm 137 sub-
mits his anger to God (notice that v. 7, the opening verse of the
final section, is specifically addressed to God). Again, it is not
explicit, but we may assume that this submission of anger to
God obviates the need for actual revenge on the enemy. I like
to think at least that Wiesel's life provides support for this
assumption. His remembrance of victimization, sustained cer-

tainly by grief and rage, is now expressed as compassion for the vulnerable and as faithfulness to God's purpose of life for all God's children. Consider Wiesel's own words:

> When I see a child, any child, I have tears in my eyes. Especially my own, especially Jewish children, but any children. That is why I can never be severe with a child. . . . We [Holocaust survivors] want to caress our children 24 hours a day. We want to shelter them, to show them nothing but joy and beauty. And yet we want them to know. . . . When I speak of life, I mean, children. To me, nothing is more sacred, nothing more divine, than a child's life. There are two absolutes, life and death. I choose life.[9]

For survivors of victimization, to express grief and rage and outrage is to live. If Wiesel's life can be taken as evidence, such expression is the first step in a life-long process of remembrance that issues ultimately in a compassion for others, grounded in God's compassion for all and God's will for life.

It is clear that a process of remembrance that develops beyond grief and anger to embrace compassion is based ultimately on forgiveness, as is God's compassion. If we are correct in assuming that vengeance submitted to God results eventually in forgiveness and compassion, then we must conclude also that Psalms 109 and 137 point finally to the cross. On the cross, God bore the pain of victimization for the sake of the victimizers—"while we still were sinners Christ died for us" (Rom. 5:8). The cross is the ultimate symbol of God's forgiveness, God's faithful compassion (*ḥesed*). It is thus appropriate that a well-known metrical version of Psalm 137 ends with a reflection on the cross:

> Let thy cross be benediction
> For men bound in tyranny;
> By the power of resurrection
> Loose them from captivity.[10]

To remember is to bear the pain of reliving an unutterable horror—a cross. But to remember is also to resist the forces of evil in the hope of living again—resurrection.

Remembrance, which is at the heart of Psalm 137, is also at the heart of the Christian faith. In instituting the sacrament of the Lord's Supper, Jesus said, "Do this in remembrance of me" (Luke 22:19). The sacrament relives or represents the pain of Jesus' death—"this is my body, which is given for you" (Luke 22:19). But the memory of Jesus' death also sustains the hope of living again—"You proclaim the Lord's death until he comes" (1 Cor. 11:26). Frederick Buechner's reflections on the importance of remembering help us to appreciate the central concept of Psalm 137.

> When you remember me, it means you have carried some-thing of who I am with you, that I have left some mark of who I am on who you are. It means that you can summon me back to your mind even though countless years and miles may stand between us. It means that if we meet again, you will know me. It means that even after I die, you can still see my face and hear my voice and speak to me in your heart.
>
> For as long as you remember me, I am never entirely lost. When I'm feeling most ghost-like, it's your remembering me that helps remind me I actually exist. When I'm feeling sad, it's my consolation. When I'm feeling happy, it's part of why I feel that way.
>
> If you forget me, one of the ways I remember who I am will be gone. If you forget me, part of who I am will be gone.
>
> "Jesus remember me when you come into your kingdom," the good thief said from his cross (Luke 23:42). There are perhaps no more human words in all of scripture, no prayer we can pray so well.[11]

We can also pray and be instructed by Psalm 137. We can pray it for victims, for those in captivity, for ourselves; as Buechner suggests, remembering has as much or more to do with the present and future as it does with the past. As we pray and reflect upon Psalm 137, we remember and are re-taught the pain of exile, the horror of war, the terror of despair and death, the loneliness of a cross. But in praying and reflect-ing upon Psalm 137, we also are taught to submit our frailty and finitude to God; we begin a journey that transforms grief and anger into compassion; we affirm that life is lived and

promised in the midst of death; we anticipate and celebrate a
resurrection power that frees us from captivity.

PSALM 82

At first glance, Psalm 82 seems quite unlike Psalms 109 and
137, and indeed, quite irrelevant to the contemporary world.
As Patrick D. Miller suggests:

> It is not a psalm that has been significant in the history of piety
> or worship. For Psalm 82 is one of the most overtly mythological
> texts in scripture, which in its form and content seems to touch
> base hardly at all with anything familiar to persons in the
> community of faith. . . . The psalm looks as if it could have come
> straight out of Canaanite mythology.[12]

Upon closer examination, however, Psalm 82 shares much in
common with Psalm 109. Both psalms involve a trial. Whereas
in Psalm 109 the psalmist puts the enemy on trial, in Psalm 82
God puts the other gods on trial. In Canaanite mythology it
was the high god El who convened the council of the gods. In
Psalm 82:1, it is Israel's God who has displaced El and who
convenes what turns out to be anything but a routine meeting.
In extraordinary fashion, Israel's God proceeds to put the
other gods on trial. After the gods are indicted (vv. 2-4), verse
5 summarizes the case and announces the verdict. On the basis
of the case against the gods, they are condemned to death (vv.
6-7). Whereas Psalm 109 represented the psalmist's desire for
retribution against an unjust enemy, Psalm 82 represents *God's*
desire for and enactment of retribution against unjust gods.

What is crucial to notice is that the psalmist's desire for
retribution in Psalm 109 and God's enactment of retribution
in Psalm 82 are based on precisely the same grounds—
namely, how the offender has treated the poor and needy (see
Ps. 109:16, where the NRSV translates the Hebrew terms *ānî*
and *ebyôn* as "poor" and "needy"; *ānî* in 82:3 appears as
"lowly" and *ebyôn* in 82:4 as "needy"). Whereas the key word
in Psalm 109 was *ḥesed*, "steadfast love," the key word in

Psalm 82 is translated "justice" (the root *špṭ* occurs four times—"judgment" in v. 1; "judge" in v. 2; "justice" in v. 3; "judge" in v. 8). The issue in both cases is the nature of divinity and the expectation that human behavior conform to God's will. The enemy in Psalm 109 failed to embody God's *ḥesed*; the gods in Psalm 82 fail to embody God's demand for justice. They "judge unjustly" (v. 2), and such behavior is grounds for conviction.

The inadequacy of such behavior is also clear in another context, in which God commands the people of Israel to "do no injustice [*āwel*] in judgment [*mišpaṭ*]" (Lev. 19:15, my translation). Such behavior is grounds for the conviction of humans as well as gods, and again the rationale centers on the nature of divinity. Leviticus 19, part of the Holiness Code, is governed by the opening exhortation, "You shall be holy; for I the LORD your God am holy" (19:2); and the recurring motivational phrase is "I am the LORD your God" (19:4, 9, 12, 14, etc.). In short, injustice among humans and certainly among gods violates the very nature of who God is and what God wills for humanity.

Verse 4 allows us to get even more specific. Justice involves the very concrete matter of how power is distributed in the human community and thus the matter of who has access to life (see again Ps. 109:16, 31, where the enemy's behavior threatens the psalmist with death). In biblical terms, only persons whose lives are threatened need to be rescued or delivered (v. 4). The psalmists frequently plead in life-threatening situations for God to rescue them, often to rescue them from the wicked (see Pss. 17:13; 71:2, 4). The word *deliver (nzl)* is used to describe what God did to save the Israelites "out of the hand of the Egyptians" (Exod. 18:10; see also "deliverance" in Pss. 33:19; 56:13). The phrase "deliver out of the hand of" is an idiomatic expression in which "hand" denotes "grasp," or more to the point, "power." In Psalm 82, the gods should have rescued and delivered the poor and needy from the power of the wicked (v. 4), but it was precisely the wicked to whom the gods have been partial (v. 2). For the God of Israel, things are right in the human community when power

is distributed in a way that all persons, especially the power-
less, have access to the resources that enable them to live.

Verse 5 describes the consequences of the gods' failure to do
justice: "All the foundations of the earth are shaken." In ancient Near Eastern cosmology, the mountains were the foundations that held up the firmament and thus kept the cosmos
together. When they were shaken, the whole creation was
threatened by the return of chaos (see Isa. 24:18-19; Ps. 46:1-3).
Thus verse 5 suggests that injustice is the undoing of creation.
Where injustice exists, the world—at least the world as God
intends it—falls apart. Injustice—any situation in which some
people live at the expense of others—is incompatible with life
as God intended it for the creation.[13] Because the gods have
sanctioned an ordering of the human community that denies
life to some persons, the gods themselves deserve to die (vv.
6-7). Psalm 82 ends with a summons to the God of Israel to
"judge the earth" (v. 8), to set things right on the earth, which
the gods have threatened with chaos (v. 5). The final verse of
Psalm 82 is a prayer, and here again, Psalm 82 is similar to
Psalm 109. As was the case with Psalm 109, the psalmist's
appeal to God in 82:8 can be stated in more familiar terms:
"Thy kingdom come, thy will be done on earth as it is in
heaven," or better translated, "Bring your kingdom, do your
will on earth as in heaven." Psalm 82:8 anticipates the prayer
that Jesus taught his disciples to pray, and Psalm 82 as a whole
anticipates Jesus' message and ministry. In a ministry to the
poor and needy, Jesus proclaimed the reign of God, which is
life as God intends it. In short, Jesus embodied the justice and
compassion that Psalms 82 and 109 (and 137) affirm is at the
heart of God's very nature.

PART IV:

INSTRUCTION FOR PROFESSION AND PROFESSION AS INSTRUCTION

CHAPTER 8

ASSURANCE: YOU ARE WITH ME

In Part III, we dealt primarily with psalms addressed to God—prayers. In Part IV, we turn to psalms that are more *about* God than addressed *to* God. To be sure, several of the psalms treated in chapters 8 and 9 do include direct address to God (Pss. 23:4-5; 73:18-28; 48:9-11; and 90 in its entirety). But more frequently God is spoken of in the third-person, and these psalms have more the character of professions of faith rather than prayers. In this chapter, we consider Psalms 23, 46, and 73 under the rubric of "Assurance." Psalms 23 and 46 affirm the presence of God with the psalmist ("with me" in Ps. 23:4; "with us" in Ps. 46:7, 11), and Psalm 73 affirms the presence of the psalmist with God ("with you" in Ps. 73:23). By offering the assurance of "God with us," these psalms reinforce the thoroughly theological understanding of reality that we encountered above; and they also anticipate the good news of Jesus Christ, who was known as Emmanuel, "God with us" (Matt. 1:23).

PSALM 23

Psalm 23 is probably the most familiar passage in the entire Old Testament and perhaps in all of Scripture. Never have I officiated at a funeral that the family failed to request that I read Psalm 23. It is remarkable in a culture in which most people rarely see sheep and have never seen a shepherd that Psalm 23 functions so pervasively and powerfully. In a real sense Psalm 23 speaks for itself; as Brueggemann puts it, "It is almost pretentious to comment on this Psalm."[1] On the other hand, the very fact of its familiarity invites the attempt to hear Psalm 23 in a fresh way.

Verses 1-3

In the context of a society and an economic system like ours, driven far more by greed than by need, the opening line of Psalm 23 is profoundly radical: "The LORD is my shepherd,/I shall not want." The sense of "I shall not want" is "I shall lack nothing," but the traditional translation is particularly apt in a culture that teaches us to *want everything*. It is difficult for us even to imagine having only the necessities of life—food, drink, shelter/protection. It is perhaps even more difficult for us to accept the message of the opening line of Psalm 23: *God is the only necessity of life!* For the psalmist, God is the only necessity of life, because God provides the other necessities— food, drink, shelter/protection. Such is the message of the remainder of verses 1-3. Contrary to the usual understanding, the sheep/shepherd imagery is not aimed primarily at communicating a sense of peace and tranquility; it is intended rather to say that God keeps the psalmist alive. For a sheep, to "lie down in green pastures" means to have food; to be led "beside still waters" means to have something to drink; to be led in "right paths" means to avoid falling in a hole or to avoid falling prey to wild animals. In short, God "restores my soul," or better translated, God "keeps me alive." As sheep owe their very lives to the shepherd, so the psalmist affirms that she or he owes her or his very life to God. God is the only necessity of life, because God provides all that is needed to sustain life "for his name's sake." God provides, because that's the way God is. It is God's fundamental character to will and faithfully to provide life for God's people.

As suggested above, it is almost impossible in our culture to communicate effectively the simple good news of Psalm 23:

God is the only necessity of life! It sounds too naive—as naive as saying that the solution to the ecological crisis is to praise God or as naive as saying that prayer is a way of life.[2] Perhaps it even sounds as naive as the words of Jesus: "Therefore I tell you, do not worry about your life, what you will eat or what you will drink, or about your body, what you will wear. . . . But strive first for the kingdom of God and his righteousness, and all these things will be given to you as well" (Matt. 6:25, 33).

In short, the only necessity of life is to live under God's reign. The proper response to the good news of Psalm 23 and the good news of Jesus Christ is trust. Like the songs of praise and like the psalmic prayers, Psalm 23 subverts the prevailing cultural creed that "our lives are our own" and that "it's all up to us." Life is not a reward to be earned; it is a gift to be accepted.

In addition to the assurance that God provides the necessities of life, there is a further dimension to the similarity between Psalm 23 and Matthew 6:25-33. The explicit grounding of God's provision in the reality of God's reign (in Matt. 6:33) is implicit in Psalm 23. In particular, the shepherd image has royal connotations. In Ezekiel 34, the shepherds of Israel are the kings, whose specific purpose is to "feed the sheep" (v. 2) and more generally to gather and care for and protect them in every way (vv. 4, 8). Ezekiel 34 indicts the kings for their failure to provide for the sheep (vv. 2-10), and it offers the assurance that God will be the shepherd of the sheep (vv. 11-16). God "will feed them with justice" (v. 16). Because God does what a ruler is supposed to do (see Ps. 72:1-4, 12-14), the reign of God is of fundamental importance. God is the only necessity of life!

Verse 4

The shepherd image continues into verse 4, which is both the structural and theological center of Psalm 23. God's provision is sufficient in even the most life-threatening situation, "the darkest valley" (NRSV) or "the valley of the shadow of death"

(RSV). The similarity between the Hebrew words for "evil" (*rā*) and "my shepherd" (*rō ʾî*) is striking and catches the reader's attention. The effect is to pit dramatically the shepherd against the threatening evil. Evil is real, to be sure, but it is not to be feared. The shepherd's provision is sufficient. The phrase "I fear no evil" is reminiscent of the central feature of the prophetic salvation oracle, which is particularly prominent in Isaiah 40–55 (see 41:11-13, 14-16; 43:1-7; 44:6-8; 54:4-8). The word *comfort* is also thematic in Isaiah 40–55 (see 40:1-2; 49:13; 51:3, 12, 19; 52:9). The historical setting of Isaiah 40–55 is that of exile, Israel's "darkest valley." The message of the prophet is that even in exile, God will provide. Indeed, the introductory oracle concludes that God "will feed his flock like a shepherd" (Isa. 40:11).

For Israel in exile and for the psalmist in her "darkest valley," God is present to provide. The central affirmation "you are with me" is made even more emphatic by the shift from third to second person in referring to God and by the presence of the pronoun "you." The direct address heightens the sense of the intimacy of God's presence. As Brueggemann points out, the presence of "you" at the center of the psalm is accompanied by the only two uses of the personal name "Yahweh" at the beginning and end of the psalm.[3] Structure reinforces content; Yahweh's presence is pervasive both in the psalm itself and in the life of the psalmist.

The "rod" in verse 4 makes sense, of course, as a shepherd's implement; however, the word even more frequently signifies royal authority and rule (Gen. 49:10; Judg. 5:14; Ps. 45:7; Isa. 14:5). What is ultimately comforting is the assurance that Yahweh is sovereign and that Yahweh's powerful presence provides for our lives. It is "this extraordinary power" that "belongs to God and does not come from us," that enables us to affirm with the apostle Paul that we may be "afflicted in every way, but not crushed; perplexed, but not driven to despair; persecuted, but not forsaken; struck down, but not destroyed" (2 Cor. 4:8). Paul knew what the psalmist knew—God is the only necessity of life!

Verses 5-6

While some interpreters attempt to discern the sheep/shepherd imagery in verses 5-6, the opinion of Kraus is much more typical: "An entirely new picture comes into view in v. 5."[4] Yahweh is now portrayed as a gracious host. In any case, whether or not the metaphor shifts is not crucial. The gracious host does for the guest exactly what the shepherd did for the sheep—he or she provides food ("You prepare a table before me"), drink ("my cup overflows"), and shelter/protection ("in the presence of my enemies"/"I shall dwell in the house of the LORD"). The host imagery articulates the very same message as the shepherd imagery—God is the only necessity of life!

Like 1-4, verses 5-6 suggest that it is God's very character to provide for God's people. The clue in verses 1-4 was the phrase "for his name's sake." The primary indication in verses 5-6 is the Hebrew word *hesed*, which the RSV and the NRSV translate as "mercy" rather than their usual "steadfast love." As suggested above, *hesed* lies at the heart of God's character; the word appears twice in God's self-revelation to Moses (Exod. 34:6-7). Israel joyfully celebrated God's *hesed* in its songs of praise (Pss. 100:5; 117:2; 118:1-4; 136:1-26; etc.) and appealed to God's *hesed* "out of the depths" (Pss. 130:7; see 13:5; 32:10; 51:1; 109:21, 26). The word for "goodness" in Psalm 23:5 is also reminiscent of God's self-revelation to Moses; it is God's "goodness" that passes before Moses in Exodus 33:19 (see also Pss. 100:5; 106:1; 107:1; 118:1; 136:1 where "goodness" and *hesed* are paired as reasons for praising God).

Most translations suggest that God's "goodness" and *hesed* will "follow" the psalmist, but the Hebrew verb *rdp* has a more active sense. The revised New American Bible is more helpful: "Only goodness and love will *pursue* me all the days of my life." God is in active pursuit of the psalmist! This affirmation is particularly striking in view of "the presence of my enemies." Ordinarily in the Psalms, it is precisely the enemies who pursue the psalmist (see 7:5; 69:26; 71:11; 109:16; etc.).

Here the enemies are present but have been rendered harm-
less, while God is in active pursuit.

The mention of "the house of the LORD" in verse 6 may
indicate the Temple and be a clue to the psalm's original cultic
use.[5] It is just as likely, however, that the "stay in the sanctuary
is . . . metaphorical for keeping close contact with the personal
God."[6] In short, the final line of the psalm is another way of
affirming that "you are with me" (v. 4), as the immediately
preceding line has also proclaimed (v. 6a).

But the mention of "the house of the LORD" may have yet
richer significance. To be in "the house of the LORD," literally
or metaphorically, provides a communal dimension to this
psalm that is usually heard exclusively individualistically.
This communal dimension is reinforced when Psalm 23 is read
in conjunction with Psalm 22, as the editors of the Psalter may
have intended. Not only can the depth of the trust expressed
in Psalm 23 be appreciated more fully after reading Psalm 22,
but also the conclusion of Psalm 22 (vv. 21-31) seems to anticipate and prepare for the ending of Psalm 23 (vv. 5-6). Psalm 22
ends with the psalmist in the "congregation" (22:22, 25), which
would have been found in "the house of the LORD" (23:6).
Perhaps also the meal mentioned in both psalms would have
taken place in "the house of the LORD" (22:26; 23:3).[7] In any
case, we are led to reflect upon what it means to be a part of
God's household. Isaac Watts's marvelous metrical version of
Psalm 23 is helpful in this regard. The third stanza, which
paraphrases verse 6, enables the reader to realize how verse 6
is a sort of summary of the whole psalm; and it also provides
an image of being "at home" with God:

> The sure provisions of my God
> Attend me all my days;
> O may Your House be my abode,
> And all my work be praise.
> There would I find a settled rest,
> While others go and come;
> No more a stranger, or a guest,
> But like a child at home.[8]

To be "a child at home" means inevitably to be a part of a family. To be "a child at home" in God's household means for us to be part of the church, a family that gathers around a table that is meant to reconcile all people, even enemies.

Two quotations from Tillie Olsen's short stories help us to appreciate the profound, indeed radical, significance of being "at home." In her story "Hey Sailor, What Ship?" Olsen focuses on an old, drunken sailor who returns periodically to the only friends he has. His cursing and his drunken ways embarrass one of the daughters of the family, and she says to her mother, "Why don't you and Daddy just kick him out of the house? He doesn't belong here." To which the mother replies, "Of course, he belongs here, he's part of us, like family. . . . Jeannie, this is the only house in the world he can come into and be around people without having to pay."[9] To be "at home," especially in God's household, is to belong and to be provided for "without having to pay" (see also Isa. 55:1-13).

In another story, Olsen specifically associates the concept of home with church. In "O Yes," Carol, a twelve-year-old girl, and her mother are the only white people at a worship service in an African-American church. They are there to see Carol's best friend be baptized, but the animated singing and shouting bother Carol. Her mother tries to explain:

> "Maybe somebody's had a hard week, Carol, and they're locked up with it. Maybe a lot of hard weeks bearing down."
> "Mother, my head hurts."
> "And they're home, Carol, church is home. Maybe the only place they can feel how they feel and maybe let it come out. So they can go on. And it's all right."[10]

Church is home! If it's true, if indeed we are "at home" in God's household, if the Lord is truly our shepherd, if God is really the only necessity of life, then the implications are profound and radical. The message of the songs of praise is reinforced. We are not our own! We belong to God and God's household; we belong to one another; our world is transformed.

M. Douglas Meeks, in his book *God the Economist*, recognizes the radical implications of Psalm 23. He concludes the final chapter quoting Aubrey R. Johnson's rendering of Psalm 23, in which verse 6 appears as follows:

> Yea, I shall be pursued in unfailing kindness
> every day of my life,
> finding a home in the Household of Yahweh
> for many a long year.[11]

Meeks understands Psalm 23 to be an articulation of the same message ultimately embodied in the Lord's Supper, which also has to do with God's free provision of food, drink, and security for life within God's household. Meeks puts it as follows:

> The celebration of the Lord's Supper is under orders from God the Economist and is a concrete instance of God's providential *oikonomia* [the Greek word from which our word *economy* is derived; it means literally "law of the household"] *with implications for all eating and drinking everywhere.* For this reason the disciples of Jesus should pray boldly for daily bread (Luke 11:13). They should keep the command to eat and drink, recognizing that it includes the command that they should share daily bread with all of God's people.
> . . . Psalm 23 depicts the work of God's economy overcoming scarcity in God's household.[12]

Psalm 23, like the Lord's Supper, becomes finally an invitation to live under God's rule and in solidarity with all of God's people. As I said at the outset, to affirm that "The LORD is my shepherd, I shall not want" is to affirm that God is the only necessity of life. It is a profoundly radical affirmation of faith that transforms us and our world. To be sure, Psalm 23 is to be heard in the midst of death, but it is also to be heard amid the not-so-ordinary daily activities of life—eating, drinking, and seeking security.

Psalm 23 and Jesus Christ

While the unity of the two metaphors—shepherd and host—
is eminently comprehensible from the language and movement of Psalm 23 itself (see also the larger Old Testament
context, especially Deut. 2:7; Neh. 9:21; Ps. 78:19), it is inevitable that Christians perceive the unity in the person of Jesus
Christ. While in no sense a prediction of the Lord's Supper,
Psalm 23:5 cannot help reminding Christians of the Lord's
Supper. Jesus is the gracious host who prepares the table that
reconciles enemies and offers life (see Mark 14:22-25; interestingly, Mark 14:27 alludes to Zech. 13:7, a passage about sheep
and shepherds). In a story with obvious eucharistic overtones
(Mark 6:30-44, especially vv. 41-42), Jesus feeds people. The
crowd is to "sit down . . . on the green grass" (v. 39), a detail
that recalls Psalm 23:2. That the allusion is not coincidental is
suggested by Mark's description of Jesus' motivation for having compassion on the crowd—"they were like sheep without
a shepherd" (v. 34). Jesus acts as both host and shepherd.

Jesus is cast even more clearly in the role of shepherd in John
10:1-17. As in Psalm 23, the shepherd leads the sheep (10:3),
providing food (10:9) and protection (10:12-13) for the purpose
of sustaining life itself (10:10). And Jesus says specifically, "I
am the good shepherd" (10:11, 14). Interesting too in John 10
is the enigmatic mention of "other sheep that do not belong to
this fold" (v. 16). Does this refer to Christians beyond the
Johannine community? Does this refer more broadly to adher-
ents of other world religions? The solution is unclear; but in
the light of the communal conclusion to Psalm 23 (especially
in view of the conclusion of Psalm 22 where "all the ends of
the earth" and "all the families of the nations" are to "turn to
the LORD" and "worship before him"; v. 27), it is worthy of
note that John 10 envisions God's household in very open
terms with room perhaps for "enemies" (Ps. 23:5) and even for
"all the families of the nations" (Ps. 22:27).

This thrust torward universality is present too in the relationship between Jesus and Psalm 23:4, "you are with me."
According to Matthew, Jesus is to be named "Emmanuel . . .

'God is with us' " (1:23). This affirmation provides a frame for the Gospel, the final words of which are "I am with you always, to the end of the age" (28:20). This final affirmation of Emmanuel is in the context of Jesus' commission to "make disciples of all nations" (28:19). God intends for God's household to include "the ends of the earth" (Ps. 22:27).

In short, in New Testament terms, Jesus is shepherd, host, Emmanuel. When Psalm 23 is heard in the context of Psalm 22 and of Jesus Christ, its profoundly radical implications are even clearer: God is "with us," but God is not ours to own; the God who shepherds us to life also gives life to the world; the table at which we are hosted is one to which the whole world is invited.

PSALM 46

Like Psalm 23, the fundamental affirmation of Psalm 46 is the assurance of God's presence. Whereas Psalm 23 emphasized this assurance by placing "you are with me" in the center of the psalm, Psalm 46 emphasizes this assurance by means of a refrain: "The LORD of hosts is with us;/ the God of Jacob is our refuge" (vv. 7, 11). The plural "with us" makes the affirmation even more explicitly corporate than in Psalm 23.

Verses 1-3

The psalm begins with a cluster of words describing God— "refuge," "strength," "help." The word *refuge (maḥăseh)* recalls the beginning of the Psalter: "Happy are all who take refuge in him [God]" (2:12). As Seybold recognizes, the root *ḥsh* becomes thematic in Psalms 1–10. Additional occurrences in 5:11 and 7:1, along with the appearance of related words, lead Seybold to conclude that "it is quite obvious that the *motif of trust* is dominant in all of these texts [Psalms 1–10], which build a chain of assorted *creedal statements.*"[13] What Seybold suggests concerning Psalms 1–10 might well be said of Books I and II of the Psalter, in which the root *ḥsh* occurs seventeen more times, including Psalm 46:1. The effect is to give the whole Psalter a creedal orientation. To take refuge in God is to live in dependence upon God alone—God is the only necessity of life! And this approach to life is founded on the fundamental conviction that God is sovereign, that God is in control—not the wicked nor the enemies nor the nations that so often threaten the life of the psalmist (see 2:1-3, 11; 7:1; 11:1-2; 25:19-20; 31:19-20; etc.). Such is the message of Psalm 2 at the beginning of the Psalter, and Psalm 46 reinforces the message.

The word *strength* underscores the conviction of God's sovereignty. It occurs twice in the Song of Moses and Miriam (Exod. 15:2, 13), which culminates in the affirmation that "the LORD will reign forever and ever" (15:18). The word also occurs frequently in the enthronement psalms that celebrate Yahweh's rule (29:1; 93:1; 96:7; 99:4). In short, Psalm 46:1 establishes the conviction that Yahweh rules the world. It may not be entirely coincidental in this regard that the following psalm is an enthronement psalm; it explicitly refers to God as "a great king over all the earth" (47:2; see vv. 6-8).

Just as Psalm 23 affirmed God's presence and rule at the extremities of life (v. 4, "the darkest valley"), so does Psalm 46. In fact, if possible, verses 2-3 present an even bleaker situation than Psalm 23—the ultimate "worst-case scenario." The "change" affecting the earth that is described in verses 2-3 seems to involve a combination of a class-five hurricane and an earthquake measuring a ten on the Richter scale. Actually, what the psalmist has in view is even worse! In the ancient Near Eastern understanding of the universe, the mountains were the foundation that both anchored dry land in a watery chaos and held up the sky. The worst possible scenario would be for the mountains to "shake" or "tremble," for dry land would be threatened from below by water and from above by the sky falling. In short, verses 2-3 are as close as the psalmist can come to a literal description of the world's falling apart. In the face of this worst case, the psalmist affirms God as "refuge," "strength," and "help." When the very structures of the universe as we know it cannot be depended upon, when our world is falling apart, God can still be depended upon. As in Psalm 23:4, the affirmation here is that "we will not fear" (v. 2).

Verses 1-3 are a remarkable affirmation of our fundamental assurance—God is the only necessity of life!

Verses 4-7

The threat, which is framed in cosmic terms in verses 2-3, is described in human terms in verse 6. The nations are in an "uproar" (v. 6), which is the same Hebrew word used to say that the waters "roar" (v. 3). The kingdoms "totter" (v. 6), which is the same Hebrew word used to say that the mountains "shake" (v. 2). It seems that everything is in motion, but there is one point of stability: "the city of God" (v. 4), in whose midst is God (v. 5). Verses 4-5 are structurally surrounded by the descriptions of movement and instability (vv. 2-3, 6). But in the midst of threatening chaos, the city of God "shall not be moved." The verb translated "moved" is the same word as "shake" in verse 2 and "totter" in verse 6. The pattern of repetition emphasizes the assurance—God's presence can be solidly depended upon.

The "city of God" is Jerusalem, in which was the Temple that represented "the holy habitation of the Most High" (v. 4). Without asserting that God was confined to Mount Zion, the prevailing theology did view Zion as Yahweh's special place. In short, the "city of God" is symbolic of God's presence.[14] The refrain summarizes the assurance—God "is with us," "our refuge" (v. 7). The Hebrew word here translated "refuge" is different from the word in verse 1, but the meaning is virtually synonymous. In the midst of international chaos, even cosmic chaos, God can be depended upon.

The significance of the "river" in verse 4 is more metaphorical than geographical. The chaotic waters of verses 2-3 have become a life-giving stream. That there is not really a river flowing through Jerusalem is no problem. This river is symbolic, like the river in Ezekiel 47:1-12, which flows from the Temple, and like the river in Revelation 22:1-2, which flows from the throne of God that has replaced the Temple in the new Jerusalem (see Rev. 21:22). Both rivers yield sustenance for life (Ezek. 47:9-12; Rev. 22:2). In short, the river in Psalm 46 seems to be another way of symbolizing the assurance of God's power and provision—God is the only necessity of life!

Verses 8-11

Verses 8 and 10 begin with imperatives, between which lies a description of God's activity (v. 9). The invitation to "Come, behold" (v. 8) may remind Christian interpreters of Philip's invitation to Nathaniel in John 1:46, "Come and see." When Nathaniel saw Jesus' works, he hailed Jesus as "the King of Israel" (John 1:49). The same movement is intended in Psalm 46, which moves toward the acknowledgment of God's sovereignty. The imperatives in verse 10*a* are explicitly instructional, "Be still, and know that I am God" (see Ps. 100:3). Although the NRSV retains it because of its familiarity, "Be still" is not a good translation. Readers tend to hear it as a call to relax or meditate, when it should be heard in the light of verse 9 as something like: "Stop!" or "Thrown down your weapons!" In other words, depend on God instead of on yourselves. The remainder of verse 10 is an explicit affirmation of God's sovereignty over the nations, who were especially in view in verses 4-6, and the cosmos, which was especially in view in verses 1-3. The verb translated "exalted" (*rûm*) is used elsewhere in the context of kingship, both of earthly kings (Num. 24:7; Ps. 89:19) and of Yahweh as king (Pss. 99:5, 9; 145:1, where the NRSV translates it as "extol," or more literally, "Cause to be exalted"). God rules over all!

In the light of the description of God's activity in verse 9, it seems that verse 8*b* may be intended as satire. The "desolations" God brings (v. 8*b*), in contrast to human efforts, involve the cessation of war and the destruction of all human implements of destruction (v. 9). This affirmation of God's sovereignty and God's will for peace among nations and in the cosmos is, as suggested in chapter 2, eschatological; it does not appear that God reigns nor that peace prevails. The eschatological orientation of Psalm 46 and the Psalter as a whole call us to a decision—in terms of Psalm 46, "Come, behold. . . . Be still, and know that I am God" (vv. 8, 10). In our day, the decision to recognize God's sovereignty is still crucial. Our implements of destruction are no longer just bows and spears and shields. We have tanks and submarines and nuclear warheads and "smart bombs" and patriot missiles. The latter are even known as "the Peace-Keeper," a revealing indication of what we depend on for security. Psalm 46 proclaims that our ultimate security rests not in our own efforts nor our own implements, but rather in the presence and power of God. Even in the "worst-case scenario," which we may be able to imagine more readily than any other generation in human history (Nuclear holocaust? Depletion of the ozone layer? etc.), God will prevail. We humans, by the assertion of our sovereignty, may be able to destroy the environment; and we may even be able to destroy human life. But we will not be able to destroy God nor ultimately thwart God's purposes. If we refuse the invitation to "know that I am God," God will simply prevail despite us rather than through us. God is the only necessity of life! Come and see!

PSALM 73

While the nature of the crisis may be different in Psalm 73 than in Psalms 23 and 46, the assurance is the same. Threatened by the "prosperity of the wicked" (v. 3) and on the brink of losing his or her faith (v. 13), the psalmist eventually reaches renewed understanding of the presence of God in his or her life.

Verses 1-12

The psalmist begins by rehearsing the traditional theology: "Truly God is good to Israel" [my translation; the Hebrew text reads, "Israel," not "upright" as in the NRSV]. But the traditional theology seems to have failed. The wicked prosper, and the psalmist's faith is shaken (vv. 2-3). Not only do the wicked seem to have it made (vv. 4-9, 12), but their good fortune is a temptation to the faithful (vv. 10-11), including the psalmist.

Verses 13-17

The central section of the psalm is an obvious turning point. The psalmist apparently has managed to keep his or her "heart clean" (v. 13; see "heart," v. 1), but has nothing positive to show for it (v. 14). Keeping the faith has been "in vain" (v. 13), and the psalmist is apparently ready to renounce God. But verse 15 marks a pivot or turning point; and not coincidentally, it is the very middle verse of the psalm. The psalmist realizes that if she or he keeps talking the same way as in the past (see vv. 13-14), he or she would be unfaithful "to the circle of your [God's] children" (v. 15). What brings the psalmist through this crisis of faith is apparently the sense of identity as a member of God's people. This sense of identity, this sense of belonging to God and thus belonging to God's people, is solidified in worship (vv. 16-17). Like Psalm 23, Psalm 73 is written in the first-person, but there is a strong communal dimension to the psalmist's experience (see above and Ps. 23:6).[15]

Verses 18-28

That verses 13-17 have indeed been the turning point of the psalm is indicated by the structure and content of this final section. Whereas in verses 1-12, the psalmist was on slippery ground (vv. 1-3) and the wicked were secure (vv. 4-12), now the wicked are on slippery ground (vv. 18-20) and the psalmist is secure (vv. 21-28). Though stated differently, the assurance is the same as in Psalms 23 and 46—God is present. Although the psalmist had been a "beast toward you" (i.e., God, v. 22; the Hebrew is 'immāk), his behavior had not separated him from God: "Nevertheless I am continually with you ['immāk]" (v. 23). God is present, and as in Psalm 23:3, God "leads" the psalmist (v. 24; NRSV "guide"; the Hebrew root is *nḥh*). The affirmation of God's presence with the psalmist is emphasized by a third occurrence of the Hebrew preposition and object 'imměkā in verse 25b, which reads literally, "and with you I have no desire on earth." The two

occurrences of the word *heart* in verse 26 recall verses 1 and
13. More fundamental than traditional notions of being "pure
in heart" (v. 1) and keeping one's "heart clean" (v. 13) is the
assurance that God is the "strength of my heart." Verses
23-26, as Brueggemann suggests, "are among the most powerful, daring and treasured in the Psalter."[16] Verses 25-26
especially are a marvelous affirmation of the good news of
assurance heard in Psalms 23, 46, 73, and throughout the
Psalter—God is the only necessity of life!

Verse 28 underscores the good news. The phrase "But for
me" recalls the psalmist's precarious position in verse 2, while
the repetition of the word *good* recalls verse 1. Now it is clear
what it really means that "God is good to Israel." It does not
mean the material prosperity enjoyed by the wicked. Rather,
the essential goodness of life is "to be near God," to make God
one's "refuge" (see Pss. 2:12; 46:1). The psalmist now knows
the truth, and the truth has set her or him free "to tell of all
your [God's] works." The final verse of the psalm recalls also
the central verse; the verb translated "tell" is the same Hebrew
verb (*spr*) used in verse 15 in the phrase "I will talk." The
psalmist's talk has changed from self-pity (vv. 13-14) to praise
(v. 28). No longer an autonomous self, the psalmist affirms
that he or she belongs to God (vv. 23-28) and belongs in the
circle of God's children (v. 15). This is the essence of happiness
(see Pss. 1:1; 2:12), assurance, and life.

The Canonical Placement and Significance of Psalm 73

There are several observations about Psalm 73 that raise the
question of the significance of its place in the Psalter. First,
Psalm 73 opens Book III. Second, while it seems to focus on the
experience of an individual "I," it introduces a book of the
Psalter that is dominated by communal psalms of lament
(Psalms 74, 79, 80, 83, and at least elements of Psalms 85 and
89). It seems likely that the experience of the "I" is offered as
a model to the whole of God's people in dealing with the
prosperity of the wicked. This model would have been particularly appropriate in the years following the exile, Israel's

"darkest valley," the experience of which the communal laments in Book III almost certainly reflect.[17]

A further observation about Psalm 73 is that it seems intentionally to recall Psalms 1 and 2. The wicked are prominent characters in Psalm 73 (vv. 1-12, esp. vv. 2 and 12) as they are in Psalm 1 (vv. 1, 5, 6). As the beginning of Psalm 73 recalls Psalm 1, the end of Psalm 73 recalls the end of Psalm 2 by way of the repetition of the word *refuge* in Psalms 2:12 and 73:28. In short, Psalm 73 is a sort of summary of what the reader of the Psalter would have learned after beginning with Psalms 1 and 2 and moving through the prayers of Psalms 3–72; that is, happiness or goodness has to do not with material prosperity and success but rather with the assurance of God's presence in the midst of all the threats and dark valleys in which the psalmists find themselves. God is the only necessity of life!

Brueggemann has recently suggested that Psalm 73 plays a crucial role in the Psalter in moving from Psalm 1 to Psalm 150. While his interpretation of Psalm 1 differs somewhat from the understanding offered above, his view of the role of Psalm 73 is helpful: "Thus, I suggest that in the canonical structuring of the Psalter, Psalm 73 stands at its center in a crucial role. Even if the Psalm is not literarily in the center, I propose that it is central theologically as well as canonically."[18]

At a prominent point in the Psalter, Psalm 73 reinforces the essential instruction already offered in Psalms 1–72: God reigns; we belong to God; no experience separates us from God; happiness or goodness means to live in dependence not upon oneself but by taking refuge in God (Pss. 2:12; 73:28). This good news is the assurance derived from the book of Psalms.

The powerful way in which Psalm 73 embodies the theological message of the Psalter, indeed the whole Bible (see esp. the book of Job, to which Psalm 73 is often compared), has made it an enduring spiritual resource for Jews and Christians. Psalm 73 was the favorite psalm of twentieth-century Jewish philosopher and theologian Martin Buber. He read it at the funeral of his best friend, Franz Rosenzweig; and both Rosenzweig and Buber chose lines from Psalm 73 to be inscribed on their tombstones (for Buber, it was vv. 23-24). Buber's own words, however, make it clear that he treasured Psalm 73 not so much as a psalm about death but as a psalm about life:

> I return today once again to this psalm that I once, in accordance with Franz Rosenzweig's wishes, spoke at his graveside.
> What is it that so draws me to this poem that is pieced together out of description, report and confession and draws me ever more strongly the older I become? I think it is this, that here a person reports how he attained to the true sense of his life experience and that this sense touches directly on the eternal.[19]

The final hymn of Charles Wesley, who wrote 6,500 hymns, was written upon his deathbed and was inspired in part by Psalm 73:25:

> In age and feebleness extreme,
> What shall a sinful worm redeem?
> Jesus, my only hope thou art,
> Strength of my failing flesh and heart;
> O, could I catch a smile from thee,
> And drop into eternity!

Obviously, Wesley has given Psalm 73 a christological interpretation, testimony to his conviction that the presence of God described in Psalm 73 was ultimately embodied in Jesus Christ, Emmanuel, "God with us."

One final matter is raised by Christian use of Psalm 73: Does the psalm offer the assurance of God's presence beyond the boundary of death? Verse 24 has often been so interpreted, especially verse 24b, "And afterward you will receive me with honor." The precise meaning is unclear, and most interpreters find no evidence here for a concept of resurrection.[20] Nevertheless, Christians cannot help being reminded that for the apostle Paul it was the resurrection of Jesus that assured him that his labor in this life was "not in vain" (1 Cor. 15:58; see Ps. 73:13-14). The powerful testimony to God's presence and power in Psalm 73 anticipates Paul's affirmation that nothing "in all creation, will be able to separate us from the love of God in Christ Jesus our Lord" (Rom. 8:39). This assurance is for our living and for our dying, as Paul points out to the Romans (14:7-8): "We do not live to ourselves, and we do not die to ourselves. If we live, we live to the Lord, and if we die, we die to the Lord; so then, whether we live or whether we die, we are the Lord's."

CHAPTER 9

GOD'S SPACE AND GOD'S TIME

In the exposition of Psalm 46 in the previous chapter, it was pointed out that "the city of God" (46:4) designates Jerusalem and is symbolic of God's presence. We focused on the concept of presence ("God with us") in chapter 8. In this chapter, we explore the concept of place as well as the related concept of time.

PSALM 48

The particularities of place and time are evident in Psalm 48, which, like Psalm 46, is a Zion Song.[1] To contemporary readers, the claims made about Jerusalem probably seem wildly extravagant or perhaps even parochial and dangerously wrong. Most of us have a very attenuated sense of the sacredness of space (although many persons will say that they somehow feel different when they enter the church sanctuary, for instance). In any case, the psalmist's claims for Jerusalem may not be nearly so strange as they initially sound. Indeed, the dynamics of faith operative in Psalm 48 are very similar to the dynamics of faith involved in the Christian profession of the centrality of Jesus of Nazareth.

Verses 1-3

The psalm begins with an affirmation of Yahweh's greatness and an implicit invitation to praise Yahweh. This praise is to take place "in the city of our God"; however, what follows immediately is not direct praise of God but rather praise of the city itself, Jerusalem, in a longer-than-usual poetic line (v. 2), which perhaps emphasizes the weightiness of the claims. As suggested above, the claims sound exaggerated, if not simply mistaken. Jerusalem does occupy a mountain, but it may be stretching it a bit to affirm that Mount Zion is "beautiful in elevation." To assert that Jerusalem "is the joy of all the earth" may well have evoked as much controversy in the ancient world as it would today. And to say that Mount Zion is "in the far north" is puzzling. Far north of what? The Hebrew word translated "north" also could be rendered as the proper name "Zaphon," the name of the mountain upon which the Canaanites believed their gods resided. This phrase seems to be a way of affirming that Yahweh has displaced the Canaanite deities (see Ps. 82:1). In any case, these assertions point toward the climatic claim that Jerusalem is "the city of the great King"—namely, Yahweh. God reigns, and Jerusalem is God's city. Within its "citadels," God has proven to be "a sure defense" (the Hebrew word is the same one the NRSV renders as "refuge" in Ps. 46:7, 11). In short, Jerusalem is the indisputable and indestructible capital of the world!

Verses 4-11

But the claim is disputed, as verse 4 makes clear, intentionally recalling verses 2-3. In contrast to the "great King" (v. 2), competing "kings assembled" (v. 4). The Hebrew for "assembled (*nô ʿădû; niphal* perfect of *yʿd*) recalls the claim of verse 3b, which could be literally translated, "God has made [Godself] known [*nôdaʿ, niphal* perfect of *ydʿ*] as a fortress." The pun serves to emphasize the contrast; the kings' *assembling* will be futile in the face of Yahweh's *revelation*. In fact, as soon as the kings *saw* Jerusalem, they were as good as defeated. The de-

scription of the kings' reaction recalls Exodus 15, the Song of
the Sea following the deliverance from the Egyptians. The
kings "were in panic" (v. 5; see "dismayed" in Exod. 15:15; see
also Ps. 2:5 where God will "terrify" the "kings of the earth");
"trembling took hold of them" (v. 6; see "trembling seized" in
Exod. 15:15) as did "anguish" (v. 6; see "pangs" in Exod.
15:14). Furthermore, the "east wind" of Psalm 48:7 recalls the
"east wind" of Exodus 14:21, which drove back the sea for the
Israelites' passage. The Song in Exodus 15:1-18 concludes with
a reference to "the mountain," which is God's "own possession" (15:17). This "place" is the one God has "established"
(15:17) and presumably the place from which God "will reign
[*yimlōk*] forever and ever" (15:18). This is precisely what Psalm
48 is about—the "great King [*melek rāb*]" (v. 2) ruling from the
city God "establishes for ever" (v. 8). The numerous allusions
in Psalm 48 to the Song of the Sea also explain the rather
curious circumstance that Jerusalem is apparently depicted as
the site of sea battle (v. 7). The battle is more metaphorical than
geographical.

The very *sight* of Jerusalem is overwhelming not only to the
assembled kings but also to approaching worshipers. What
the worshipers have "*seen* in the city of the Lord of hosts" (v.
8; see v. 5) has a profound effect on their sense of space and
time. The present sight of Jerusalem connects their experience
with the particular deliverance from Egypt and with God's
universal dominion "to the ends of the earth" (v. 10; see v.
2)—the spatial extension of God's reign. The present sight of
Jerusalem takes the worshiper back in time to the exodus but
also forward in time to Jerusalem's establishment "for ever"
(v. 8; see vv. 13-14)—the temporal extension of God's reign.
Robert Alter aptly sums up the perspective of Psalm 48: "Thus,
the towering ramparts of the fortress-city became a nexus for
all imagined time and space."[2]

One further link between Psalm 48 and Exodus 15 is the
occurrence of the word *hesed*, "steadfast love," in both texts
(Ps. 48:9; Exod. 15:13). In Exodus 15, it is God's guidance in
"steadfast love" that brings the people to God's "holy abode";
and in Psalm 48, it is precisely "steadfast love" that the people

think about "in the midst of your temple." As suggested previously, the word *ḥesed* describes God's fundamental character. As the experience of exodus and deliverance revealed God's fundamental character, so the present experience in Jerusalem puts the worshiper in touch with God's historical (past) and enduring (future) essence.

Verses 12-14

In the final three verses of the psalm, the worshipers are invited or commanded to consider Jerusalem in all its concrete architectural detail—"towers," "ramparts," "citadels" (see v. 3). Perhaps it is helpful to think of Psalm 48 recording the impressions of a worshiper as she proceeds toward the city. Whereas in verses 1-2 the worshiper admires Jerusalem from afar, now she is at the top of the mountain and is in position to see things more closely and more clearly. The five imperatives in verses 12-13 are not simply an invitation to tour the city. Much more is at stake, as is emphasized by the repetition of the Hebrew root *spr* in verses 12-13. In the third and central of the five imperatives, worshipers are invited to "count" (*siprû*) Jerusalem's towers so that they may "tell" (*tesappĕrû*) the next generation about their God. Robert Alter's translation captures the pun: "*count* its towers . . . so you may *recount*/ to the last generation:/ That this is God, our God, forever."[3] In short, observation of spatial detail leads to proclamation about God. God is "our God forever and ever" (v. 14)—the temporal extension of God's reign. God "will be our guide forever" (v. 14)—the spatial extension of God's reign as Israel is led from place to place.

This movement in verses 12-14, emphasized by the repetition of *spr* ("count, recount"), is remarkable testimony to the power of sacred space. The seemingly simple matter of seeing Jerusalem leads to the powerful proclamation of God's reign in all times and places.

The Message and Significance of Psalm 48

What are we contemporary readers to make of Psalm 48? We know that Jerusalem was not indestructible; hostile kings and armies were not put to flight by the very sight of Jerusalem. Jerusalem was destroyed in 587 B.C. by the Babylonians, for instance, and in A.D. 70 by the Romans. Was the psalmist simply mistaken? Was her or his perception blurred by an overly zealous nationalism? Was the psalmist on the payroll of the Jerusalem Chamber of Commerce? So the cynic might conclude. But before dismissing the psalmist as either a naive optimist or a misguided patriot or a clever advertiser, we must remember that the details of Psalm 48 are as much metaphorical as geographical, or at least a subtle mixture of the metaphorical and geographical. What Psalm 48 embodies is "poetic form used to reshape the world in light of belief."[4] In this case, Jerusalem, a seemingly ordinary place, has become to the eye of faith "the city of the great King" (v. 2), a powerful symbol of God's reign in all places (vv. 2, 10) and in all times (v. 14). In effect, the psalmist has created in poetic form an alternative worldview, a new reality, which for the psalmist and all the faithful has become the deepest and most profound reality of all—God rules the world, now and forever! Psalm 48 articulates the faith that no power on earth, nor the passage of any amount of time, can ultimately thwart the just and righteous purposes of God for the world (the words *victory* and *judgments* in verses 10 and 11 could also be translated "righteousness" and "justice"; see also Psalm 122 below).

The spirit of Psalm 48 is captured eloquently in a novel by Elie Wiesel:

JERUSALEM: the face visible yet hidden, the sap and blood of all that makes us live or renounce life. The spark flashing in the darkness, the murmur rustling through shouts of happiness and joy. A name, a secret. For the exiled, a prayer. For all others, a promise. Jerusalem: seventeen times destroyed yet never erased. The symbol of survival. Jerusalem: the city which miraculously transforms man into pilgrim; no one can enter it and go away unchanged.[5]

The psalmist knew precisely this about Jerusalem: "No one can enter it and go away unchanged." It is not because Jerusalem is literally indestructible or universally acclaimed, but rather because for believers, Jerusalem becomes a spatial, temporal symbol for the reality of God's rule in all times and places. Thus the footsteps of pilgrims approaching this particular place at any particular moment "reverberate to infinity."[6]

If this sounds strange to Christian readers of the Psalms, we need only consider how the same paradox, the same scandal of particularity, lies at the heart of Christianity as well. For Christians, a particular event in time (the crucifixion of Jesus) at a particular place (Golgotha) becomes the central event of history. What appeared to be an ordinary execution of a common criminal is for Christians the focal point of all space and time. In a way just as particularist and strange and scandalous as the Zion theology of Psalm 48, Christians profess the *incarnation* of God in Jesus, a first-century Jew from an out-of-the-way place called Nazareth. Essentially what we proclaim is "Christ crucified, a stumbling block to Jews and foolishness to Gentiles, but to those who are the called, both Jews and Greeks, Christ the power of God and the wisdom of God" (1 Cor. 1:23-24). What Psalm 48 and Elie Wiesel say about Jerusalem is what Christians profess about Jesus—one cannot confront him and go away unchanged. Indeed, the early followers of Jesus were known as ones "who have been turning the world upside down" (Acts 17:6).[7]

To be sure, neither the theology of Psalm 48 nor the Christian proclamation of Jesus is a facile utopianism. The psalmists knew, the apostles knew, and we still know that we humans live in time and space as part of a world that is fragile and troubled, terrified and terrifying. Yet, in the midst of it all, we join the psalmist in proclaiming a new reality—God rules the world! And what's more, we claim to live by that reality above all others. For the psalmist, the vision of Jerusalem, the city of God, reshaped time and space. For Christians, the life, death, and resurrection of Jesus of Nazareth has reshaped the world—reshaped our time and space into a new reality. Thus, amid the same old realities of trouble and turmoil, we are able to discern by the eye of faith the dimensions of "a new creation" (2 Cor. 5:17). In short, we live eschatologically (see chap. 2).

Two more psalms—one about God's space (Psalm 122) and one about God's time (Psalm 90)—will deepen our understanding of how the discernment of God's space and time affects the life of faith in our place and time.

PSALM 122

Psalm 122 is part of a collection of psalms that share the title "A Song of Ascents" (Psalms 120–134). Each psalm is relatively short, and a variety of themes is represented. Both of these features of the collection create the impression that Psalms 120–134 were used as a sort of pilgrim hymnal. The Hebrew word translated "ascents" can more literally mean "steps" or "stairs" (*ma'ălâ*), and it is used elsewhere for the steps of the Temple (Ezek. 40:6) and the steps to the city of David (Neh. 3:15; 12:37). While certainty is not possible, it is likely that the title "Song of Ascents" or "Song of the Steps" means that these songs were sung on the way up to Jerusalem. As Psalm 122:4 points out, it was decreed (see Deut. 16:16) that the "tribes go up" (Hebrew *lh*, the root from which "ascents," "steps" is formed) regularly to Jerusalem. In any case, the title "Song of Ascents" seems particularly appropriate for Psalm 122, another Zion Song that explicitly describes a visit to Jerusalem.

As in Psalm 48, architectural features of the city are prominent in Psalm 122—"the house of the Lord" (vv. 1, 9), "gates" (v. 2), "thrones" (v. 5), "walls" (v. 7), "towers" (v. 7). There is something powerful about this particular space. As is appropriate for a psalm featuring architectural details, the architecture of the psalm itself is significant. For instance, references to "the house of the Lord" encompass the psalm (vv. 1, 9), as if to say that the beginning and end, the motivation and destination, of the ascent to Jerusalem is the Temple, God's house. At the same time, there is a focusing of attention toward the

center of the psalm by means of a chiastic structure and the
repetition of the word *house:*

A	vv. 1-2	the psalmist and his companions ("I"/"us") and "house of the Lord"
B	vv. 3-4	Jerusalem
C	v. 5	"house of David"
B¹	vv. 6-7	Jerusalem
A¹	vv. 8-9	the psalmist and his companions and "house of the Lord"

There were two houses in Jerusalem—"the house of the
Lord" and "the house of David"—just as Jerusalem was
known as both "the city of God" and "the city of David." The
structure of Psalm 122 calls attention to both houses. While the
"house of David" is central, its position in the psalm and thus
its authority are encompassed by "the house of the Lord."
David's power is derivative. The three occurrences of the key
word *house* (vv. 1, 5, 9) recall the narrative of 2 Samuel 7 in
which *house* is also a key word. Second Samuel 7 makes it clear
that David did not build the Lord a house; rather, the Lord
built David a house. David's reign is but an agency of God's
reign, and the purpose of David's administration is to enact
the fundamental purpose of God's rule—justice (v. 5; NRSV
"judgment"; see Ps. 48:11). The enthronement psalms, which
celebrate God's reign, describe God's purpose as "justice."
Indeed, "righteousness and justice are the foundation of his
[God's] throne" (Ps. 97:2; see also occurrences of the noun
mišpāṭ, "justice," or verbal forms of the root *špṭ,* "judge, establish justice," in Pss. 96:10, 13; 97:8; 98:9; 99:4; see also Ps. 82:1,
2, 3, 8). In short, David's reign is to manifest God's reign. As
in Psalm 48, to experience Jerusalem is ultimately to experience the reality of God's reign and God's purpose for the
world.

Another Hebrew word often used to describe God's purpose
for the world is *shalom,* "peace" (see Pss. 29:10-11; 72:1-7),
which becomes the key word in verses 6-8. It occurs three
times, once in each verse. The Hebrew root also is a compo-

nent of the name "Jerusalem," which may mean "possession of peace" or "foundation of peace." The occurrence of the root *šlm*, along with an occurrence of the root *š'l*, "pray" (v. 6), and two occurrences of the root *šlh/šlw* ("prosper," v. 6; "security," v. 7), make for striking alliteration in verses 6-7, transliterated as follows:

> v. 6 *ša'ǎlû šĕlôm yĕrûšālām yišlāyû 'ōhǎbāyik*
> v. 7 *yehî-šālôm bĕhêlēk šalwâ be'armĕnôtāyik*

The alliteration emphasizes further the concept of "peace."

The imperative "Pray for the peace of Jerusalem" has a remarkably contemporary relevance, given the ongoing turmoil in the Middle East. In fact, Jerusalem has seldom been peaceful; and the psalmist's invitation is at least implicit recognition of Jerusalem's turmoil, the world's turmoil. The literary context reinforces this recognition; in Psalm 120, which opens the Songs of Ascents, the psalmist laments the lack of peace. In this context, the psalmist's exclamations of peace within Jerusalem (vv. 7-8) and resolve to "seek your [Jerusalem's] good" (v. 9) amount to the recognition of God's reign and his or her commitment to live under God's reign. As in Psalm 48, this commitment is not facile optimism nor mere wishful thinking. This commitment is eschatological. For the psalmist, to enter Jerusalem *really does* mean to enter a new world. The joy is real (v. 1). To live for God's sake (v. 9) and for the sake of others (v. 8) is to experience, embody, and extend the justice God intends for the world. This life-style, this commitment *is* reality. To be sure, the same old, so-called realities are still present—hatred and war (see Ps. 120:6-7), trouble and turmoil—but they are no longer determinative.

What it means to enter Jerusalem, to live eschatologically, to live under God's reign, is illustrated powerfully by one of Walker Percy's characters, Will Barrett, in the novel *The Second Coming*. Will's father committed suicide when Will was a young man, and Will's own life has been a persistent battle with a voice inside him (his father's voice, perhaps) that tells him to do the same. The voice knows what the world is like:

Come, what else is there [except suicide]? What other end if you don't make the end? Make your own bright end in the darkness of this dying world, this foul and feckless place, where you know as well as I that nothing ever really works, that you were never once yourself and never will be or he himself or she herself and certainly never once we ourselves together. Come, close it out before it closes you out because believe me life does no better job with dying than with living. Close it out. At least you can do that, not only not lose but win, with one last splendid gesture defeat the whole foul feckless world.[8]

Will's answer to the voice is a simple "no," based on the experience of genuine love between himself and another human being, which he takes as a sign that "the Lord is here."[9]

What the psalmist saw in Jerusalem was a sign that "the Lord is here," amid the dark daily realities of a dying world, a world where nothing ever works out completely right and we are never all that we can be. Walker Percy does not take the story of Will Barrett beyond his discovery of the sign, but the reader assumes that Will discontinues his frantic search for the second coming of Christ and begins to live in the new world created by the good news that "the Lord is here."

That good news is the fundamental message of Psalm 122, which is appropriately used by the church during the season of Advent. Advent maintains a dual focus on Christ's second coming and Christ's first coming, and so effectively celebrates the good news that "the Lord is here" and will be here forever. In short, like Psalm 48 and Psalm 122, the celebration of Advent affirms the extension of God's rule in space and time. God rules the world, now and forever.

PSALM 90

The dimension of time is even more prominent in Psalm 90. As suggested above, Psalm 90 occupies a crucial place in the Psalter. After Books I–III have documented the failure of the Davidic covenant, Psalm 90 opens Book IV, the "theological heart" of the Psalter with its emphasis on God's reign.[10] It is particularly interesting, given the placement of Psalm 90, that it is the only psalm in the entire Psalter that is attributed to Moses. In a sense, Moses' career centered on the problem of space—namely, getting Israel out of one place (Egypt) to another place (the Promised Land). In the final analysis, however, Moses' problem was *time*—namely, he ran out of it. In what has to be one of the most incredibly surprising aspects of the whole biblical story, the illustrious Moses dies before entering the Promised Land. The reason given is that God was "angry" with Moses (see Deut. 3:26, where the word *angry* is the same Hebrew root as the word *wrath* in Ps. 90:9, 11). At any rate, Moses becomes a paradigm for Israel's existence and for human existence. We always run out of time. Never will we fully accomplish what we would like to accomplish nor be what we would like to be. What initially seems like a depressing message, however, is actually an encouraging one. If the great Moses came up short, then perhaps it's not such a disaster that we shall too. Moses' death was a reminder that it was God, not Moses, who would lead the people into the land (see Deut. 31:3; 32:52). *Our* time, therefore, is not all there is to measure. *God's time* is primary, and as Psalm 90 suggests, our time must be measured finally in terms of God's time.

Verses 1-2

Although Psalm 90 focuses primarily on time, it begins with an affirmation involving place and time: "Lord, you have been our dwelling place in all generations." If Psalm 90 and the Psalter as a whole are intended in part to respond to the crisis of exile and the failure of the Davidic covenant, then Psalm 90:1 is a particularly pertinent and powerful affirmation. God is really the only place that counts. The land is not indispensable, the temple is not indispensable, because *God* is our dwelling place. Subsequent psalms in Book IV will affirm that God reigns (Psalms 93; 95–99), suggesting also that the Davidic monarchy is not indispensable. In short, God is the only necessity for the life of God's people and the life of the world. Such has always been the case—"in all generations" (v. 1). The word *generations* obviously implies the passage of time, but so do the two verbs in verse 2, both of which are used elsewhere in relation to child-birth. A more accurate translation of verse 2 would be as follows:

> Before the mountains were born,
>   or you had brought forth in labor
>   the earth and the world,
> from everlasting to everlasting, you are God.[11]

Here God is portrayed not as Mother Earth, but rather as mother of the earth. This God will always be the only necessity for the life of God's people and the life of the world, for God is "from everlasting to everlasting."

Verses 1-2 have already made the crucial juxtaposition of our time ("all generations") with God's time ("everlasting to everlasting"). The chiastic structure of these two verses is striking, especially considering that the use of the Hebrew pronoun ("you" in vv. 1, 2) is often for emphasis:[12]

> a   "Lord, *you*..." (God)
> b   "all generations" (time)
> c   "mountains" (space)
> c[1] "earth and the world" (space)
> b[1] "everlasting to everlasting" (time)
> a[1] "*you* are God" (God)

The literary structure makes a theological point. The divine "You" is all-encompassing of time ("generations") and space ("earth and the world"). Human life and the life of the world find their origin and destiny in God.

Verses 3-6

The language of these verses continues to call to mind the passage of time—"back to dust" (v. 3); "children" (v. 3, RSV; NRSV "mortals"); "years" (v. 4); "yesterday" (v. 4); "watch in the night" (v. 4); "morning" (vv. 5, 6); "evening" (v. 6). The poetic structure makes emphatic the reality of human transience. In verse 4, which Alter suggests "is one of the most exquisite uses of intraverset [a verset is one component of a poetic line; v. 4 contains three versets] focusing in the Bible,"[13] the movement from God's time to human time highlights the juxtaposition already begun in verses 1-2. For God, a thousand years are like three hours!

The focusing in verse 4—thousand years, yesterday, watch in the night—leads directly into verses 5-6, whose chiastic structure has the effect of re-creating the progression of a day:

> v. 5*a* "like a dream" (night)
> v. 5*b* morning
> v. 6*a* morning
> v. 6*b* evening

Poetic structure imitates the inexorable passage of time, which is precisely what Psalm 90 is about.

Verse 3 is usually taken to be an allusion to Genesis 3:19, and it may be; however, the Hebrew word for "dust" (*dakkā*) here is different from the one in Genesis 3:19 (*āpār*). It appears to mean something like "crushed, pulverized (particle)," perhaps suggesting the crushing weight of time upon human existence. As if the reality itself were not enough, God is portrayed as saying, "Turn back, you mortals." God seems almost cruel in speeding the process along; however, the word *turn* (*šûb*), used twice in verse 3, can also mean "repent." While verse 3 is unremittingly realistic about human finitude and transience, it anticipates the good news of verse 13, where God is called upon to "turn" or "repent."

Verses 7-12

Like verse 3, verses 7-12 are often interpreted in the light of Genesis 2–3. Indeed both, Psalm 90 and Genesis 2–3 do seem to describe a relationship between sin and death; however, that relationship is very difficult to define precisely. For instance, in Genesis 2–3, it is not at all clear that the humans would have lived forever if they had not sinned. According to the text, the punishment for sin was not physical death but banishment from the garden (Gen. 3:23). It is entirely possible to conclude from the text that physical death was always a part of God's plan for human life and the life of the world. This is the interpretation I prefer, although admittedly, it is not the majority position.

Returning to Psalm 90, the question is this: If death is not punishment for sin, what does Psalm 90 mean by associating human transience with the anger and wrath of God in verses 7, 9, and 11? Miller provides a helpful beginning:

> [Psalm 90] does not mean that we have to deal with a capricious, arbitrary God who may not like us or who turns our life into absurdity by cutting short our days. It does mean that the one who is the ground of our being has created for us lives that manifest love and righteousness, that continue the good purposes for which God has brought the universe into being; and that the universal failure so to live places our lives under the limitation and judgment of death.[14]

The phrase "judgment of death" need not mean physical death. In biblical terms, death means fundamentally to be alienated from God. In this sense, sin always results directly in death. The first humans sinned; they alienated themselves from God against God's intention; and so do we. Therefore, physical death becomes a problem. If we accepted our lives as a gift of God, and if we entrusted the future of our lives and the life of the world to God, then physical death would be no problem. It could be accepted as part of God's plan. But in the presence of sin, human transience is a problem. Failing to trust God, we fear physical death, and the fear of death itself becomes death-serving.[15] That is, it further alienates us from God. Thus, while sin and death are related, the relationship is not necessarily causal. Sin does not cause physical death. Rather, sin involves alienation from God, which makes physical death a problem. And when physical death is feared, then it becomes necessary to conclude that death causes sin!

Support for my interpretation may be found in verse 12. If the days of our lives are relatively brief at best and "only toil and trouble" (v. 10), then it would be insufferably sadistic of

God to "teach us to count our days" (v. 12). But verse 12 is obviously meant to be hopeful and encouraging. God is not being implored to teach us to consider how oppressive our lives are, but rather to teach us how to accept the time we've been given as a *gift!* When this is done, when life is accepted as a gift and entrusted to God, then a "wise heart" is gained and physical death is no longer a problem. Human transience—the reality of death as part of God's plan—becomes not an occasion for despair but an opportunity for prayer.

Verses 13-17

Verse 12 has marked a transition. While the entire psalm has been addressed to God, the prayer takes on an obviously different tone at verse 13. The imperative "Turn, O Lord!" recalls verse 3 where *turn* was used twice. There God's turning contributed to human transience. Verse 13 suggests that God's turning may take a different form. Verse 13 is not a request to undo human transience, for that is part of God's plan. Rather, verse 13 is a request for God to forgive human sinfulness, which alienates us from God and makes finitude a problem. The request is a bold one! God is being asked to do what sinful humans consistently fail to do—to turn or repent! The alienation caused by *human* sinfulness must be overcome by *God's* turning toward humanity, which is precisely what God's "steadfast love" (*hesed*, v. 14) is all about. Verses 13-14 recall Exodus 32–34, where Moses boldly requests God to repent (Exod. 32:12); and God does (32:14), thus revealing that God's fundamental character involves "steadfast love" (Exod. 34:6-7), which takes concrete form in the forgiveness of sin.

God's faithfulness in the face of human unfaithfulness is redemptive. In this case, God redeems time. Verses 13-17, like verses 1-12, are still a prayer about time; but the perspective on time has been remarkably transformed. Whereas previously the passage of time could be perceived only as "toil and trouble" (v. 10), now there are new possibilities. Because God is faithful, "morning" can "satisfy" (v. 14) rather than mark a fleeting moment on the way to our demise. Because

God is faithful, "days" and "years" allow us to "rejoice and be glad" (v. 14; see v. 15).

The occurrence of the word *children* in verse 16 also recalls verse 3, and again the perspective has been transformed. Whereas "children" (NRSV "mortals") in verse 3 are involved in the dissolution of life, "children" in verse 16 represent the continuity of human life. There will be a future! And as has always been the case, that future belongs first to God. It is God's work that humans need to perceive (v. 16) and upon which humans depend. To be sure, humans have work to do, but "the work of our hands" is the object of God's activity— God must "establish" it (v. 17, RSV; NRSV "prosper"). The priority of God's activity and the priority of God's time reshape human activity and human time. Our days and years are not simply moments to be endured on the way to oblivion; our efforts are not simply fleeting and futile. Because God is eternal and faithful and eternally faithful in turning toward humanity, our allotted time becomes something meaningful, purposeful, joyful, even enduring. In the final analysis, Psalm 90 functions like the songs of praise as a call to decision. We are called to entrust ourselves and our allotted time to God with the assurance that, grounded in God's work and God's time, our lives and labors participate in the eternal (see John 3:16-17, where trust in God's forgiving love results in "eternal life"). Psalm 90 is finally, therefore, not an act of futility but an act of faith. And it is also an act of hope. Without having to see it happen, the psalmist trusts that God can and will satisfy and make glad and make manifest God's work and establish the work of our hands (vv. 14-17). And Psalm 90 is also an act of love. The psalmist's trust puts him or her in communion with past generations who found a dwelling place in God (v. 1) and with future generations, the children, to whom the work of God will be manifest (v. 16). For the psalmist, sin and death are inevitable realities. But so are forgiveness and life! Psalm 90 is a profession of faith that invites us and instructs us to live the only way it makes any sense whatsoever to live—in faith and in hope and in love. The words of Reinhold Niebuhr provide an excellent summary of the good news of Psalm 90:

Nothing that is worth doing can be achieved in our lifetime; therefore we must be saved by hope. Nothing which is true or beautiful or good makes complete sense in any immediate context of history; therefore we are saved by faith. Nothing we do, however virtuous, can be accomplished alone; therefore we are saved by love. No virtuous act is quite as virtuous from the standpoint of our friend or foe as it is from our standpoint. Therefore, we must be saved by the final form of love which is forgiveness.[16]

CONCLUSION

THE PSALMS AND JESUS CHRIST

At numerous points in the previous nine chapters, I have called attention to ways in which the theological content of the Psalms is related to the message of the New Testament. Indeed, the "theological heart" of the Psalter is essentially the same as Jesus' fundamental proclamation—the Lord reigns! In addition, the New Testament writers were convinced that the Psalms bore witness to Jesus. For instance, in Luke's account of the resurrection appearances, Jesus says to the disciples, "These are my words that I spoke to you while I was still with you—that everything written about me in the law of Moses, the prophets, and the psalms must be fulfilled" (24:44). We may understand the fulfillment spoken of in Luke 24:44 to mean that the Psalms instruct us about God, the same God whom we Christians profess is revealed in an ultimate way in Jesus Christ. In any case, given the New Testament writers' conviction that the Psalms bear witness to Jesus in some way, it is not surprising that the early church sang the Psalms (see Col. 3:16) and that the Psalter is the Old Testament book that is quoted most frequently in the New Testament.[1] As Kraus puts it, "Anyone who explores the nuances of the ways in which Old Testament Psalms are used in the New Testament will be amazed at the ways in which Israel's songs of prayer and praise were alive and present in the early church."[2] To illustrate the truth of Kraus's statement, I shall focus upon the

Gospel accounts of Jesus' life and death to demonstrate how the Psalms are quoted or alluded to at crucial moments in the story.

THE BIRTH OF JESUS

In Luke's account of the birth of Jesus, a heavenly messenger or angel appears to shepherds to announce the event (2:8-12). Then the messenger is joined by "a multitude of the heavenly host" (2:13), who proclaim: "Glory to God in the highest heaven,/ and on earth peace among those whom he favors!" (2:14). While this proclamation is not a quotation of Psalm 29, it is certainly reminiscent of this enthronement psalm, in which "heavenly beings" are enjoined to "ascribe to the Lord glory and strength" (v. 1; see also v. 2). After a rehearsal of the power of the Lord's voice in verses 3-9, the heavenly beings do as they were invited: "In his temple all say 'Glory' " (v. 9). Psalm 29 concludes with an affirmation of Yahweh's kingship (v. 10) and a line that can be translated either as an affirmation of or a prayer for peace among God's people (v. 11). In short, the proclamation of the heavenly beings in Luke 2 is essentially the same as that in Psalm 29—glory to God, the correlate of which is peace among God's people.[3]

By alluding to Psalm 29 or at least by preserving the same movement as in Psalm 29, the Gospel writer makes a powerful theological affirmation. God is being enthroned in the birth of Jesus! Jesus will not only proclaim the reign of God but will embody the reign of God. In this sense, Jesus is a fulfillment of the central theological affirmation of the Psalter.

THE BAPTISM AND TEMPTATION OF JESUS

The Gospel of Mark records that at the baptism of Jesus, "a voice came from heaven, 'You are my Son, the Beloved; with you I am well pleased' " (1:11). The speech of the heavenly voice is composed of two Old Testament references. The first is a quotation of Psalm 2:7, "You are my son." Mark thus claims for Jesus the role of Messiah or Christ, "anointed one" (see Ps. 2:2; Mark 1:1). Jesus' kingship will be a fulfillment of what God intended for the institution of monarchy in Israel and Judah. That the reign of Jesus Messiah will be different is signaled clearly by the second part of the divine speech in Mark 1:11, which alludes to Isaiah 42:1, one of the four Servant Songs found in Isaiah 40–55. By juxtaposing Psalm 2:7 and Isaiah 42:1, Mark offers a new understanding of kingship. King Jesus will be a suffering servant. The heavenly voice thus anticipates the remainder of Mark's story of Jesus, especially the crucifixion, where Mark emphasizes that Jesus is king (see Mark 15:2, 9, 12, 18, 25, 32; see also v. 39). As with the story of Jesus' birth, the Gospel writers understand the significance of Jesus' baptism as a fulfillment of the Psalms.

The story of Jesus' temptation also includes a quotation from the Psalms. Interestingly, the voice quoting the Psalms in this case is not God but "the devil," who tempts Jesus to throw himself down from the pinnacle of the temple by quoting the assurances contained in Psalm 91:11-12. Jesus refuses to claim this assurance. The devil's use of the Psalms and Jesus' response are instructive. The fulfillment of the Psalms is not to be sought as Jesus pursues his own agenda or his own self-gratification. Jesus will eventually claim the assurance contained in the Psalms, but he will do so only *from the cross* (Luke 23:46, a quote from Ps. 31:5; see below).

THE TEACHING AND MINISTRY OF JESUS

Not only was the fundamental content of Jesus' teaching essentially the same as the central theological affirmation of the Psalter, but also certain specifics of Jesus' teaching are closely related to the Psalms. One example must suffice—the Beatitudes in Matthew. Like the Psalms, the Beatitudes are specifically presented as instruction (Matt. 5:2). The setting on the mountain (5:1) obviously recalls Sinai and the giving of the Torah to Moses, but the form of the Beatitudes ("Blessed are . . . ") is more reminiscent of Psalms 1:1 and 2:12. At least one of the Beatitudes is clearly derived from a psalm, and two others probably are. Matthew 5:5, with its announcement that

the "meek . . . will inherit the earth," is based on the first line
of Psalm 37:11: "But the meek shall inherit the land." Matthew
5:4 ("Blessed are those who mourn") may be based on Psalm
126:5-6, and Matthew 5:8 ("Blessed are the pure in heart") may
be derived from Psalm 24:3-4 or 73:1, 13, 28.[4]

In addition to Jesus' teaching, certain events in Jesus' ministry are remembered with reference to the Psalms. For instance,
Jesus' cleansing of the Temple, which appears in all four Gospels (Matt. 21:12-16; Mark 11:15-16; Luke 19:45-48; John 2:13-
22), is specifically understood by John as a fulfillment of Psalm
69:9, "For zeal for thy house has consumed me" (see John 2:17).
By including this event at the beginning of the Gospel rather
than toward the end as in the Synoptics, John intends to anticipate Jesus' suffering and death (see John 2:18-22). Psalm 69 is
helpful in this regard, because it is the prayer of a righteous
person who is persecuted and hated "without cause" according to verse 4, which John will also quote toward the end of the
Gospel (15:25).

A pattern is beginning to emerge. Crucial events and aspects
of Jesus' life—birth, baptism, temptation, teaching, and ministry—are not remembered nor fully understood without recourse to the Psalms. This pattern becomes even more
pronounced as the Gospels relate the story of Jesus' death and
the events leading up to the crucifixion. Particularly important
are Psalms 118 and 22.

JESUS' ENTRY INTO JERUSALEM: PSALM 118

According to the Gospels, when Jesus entered Jerusalem
shortly before his crucifixion, he was greeted by a crowd in a
manner reminiscent of Psalm 118. In Mark, the first part of the
greeting is as follows:

> "Hosanna!
> Blessed is the one who comes in
> the name of the Lord!" (Mark 11:9)

The word *hosanna* is a Hebrew word that means "Save us, we beseech you"; it occurs in Psalm 118:25. The next part of the greeting is a quotation of the first line of Psalm 118:26.

The use of Psalm 118 at this point in the story of Jesus is not really surprising. After all, Jesus enters Jerusalem during the week of Passover; and Psalm 118 is the concluding psalm of the Hallel collection (Psalms 113–118,) which were (and are) traditionally used at Passover. But this observation does not exhaust the significance of Mark's use of Psalm 118. Verses 22-23 of the psalm were understood within first-century Judaism to refer to the Messiah.[5] In fact, Matthew 21:42 cites these verses to suggest that Jesus is the rejected Messiah (see also Luke 20:17; Acts 4:11-12). In the story of Jesus' entry into Jerusalem, the Gospel writers have extended the messianic interpretation of Psalm 118 to verses 25-26. Mark 11:10 and Matthew 21:9 make this clear by mentioning "the Kingdom of our father David" and "Son of David" respectively, while the parallel accounts in Luke and John record that the crowd addressed Jesus as "King" (Luke 23:38; John 12:13). For all the Gospel writers, Psalm 118 is a means of understanding and articulating the significance of Jesus.

But even the messianic interpretation of Psalm 118 does not exhaust the significance of its use in the Gospels. While the setting-in-life of Psalm 118 in ancient Israelite worship is uncertain, it is eminently clear that Psalm 118 is a prayer for continuing salvation (v. 25), based on the recollection of past deliverances (v. 21), especially the exodus and the return from exile. The relationship to the exodus is most obvious in verse 14, which quotes the song that Moses and the Israelites sang after the crossing of the sea (Exod. 15:2*a*). The next line of the Israelites' song (Exod. 15:2*b*) is alluded to in Psalm 118:28; and both texts mention the Lord's "right hand" three times in celebrating deliverance (Exod. 15:6, 12; Ps. 118:15, 16). Furthermore, the summary of the crossing of the sea (Exod. 14:30-31), which introduces the Israelites' song, contains several words that occur with the same sense in Psalm 118 ("save" in Exod. 14:30 and Ps. 118:14, 21, 25; "day" in Exod. 14:30 and Ps. 118:24; "saw" in Exod. 14:30 and Ps. 118:7). Without a doubt,

Psalm 118 should be heard in the light of Exodus 14–15. The allusion to the return from exile is not as prominent, but it is revealing that Psalms 106, 107, and 136, all of which begin with the same two lines as Psalm 118, conclude by linking God's saving activity with the return from exile. In short, both the exodus and the return from exile are manifestations of the goodness and steadfast love that all worshipers of the Lord are invited to celebrate (see vv. 1 and 29, which begin and end the psalm, as well as vv. 2-4).[6]

This observation is the clue to the ultimate significance of the use of Psalm 118 by the Gospel writers. By articulating the significance of Jesus through Psalm 118, they profess that the life, death, and resurrection of Jesus are an extension or further fulfillment of God's saving activity in the exodus and the return from exile. Quite properly, Psalm 118 has become in church tradition not just a psalm for Palm Sunday, which celebrates Jesus' entry into Jerusalem, but also for Easter Sunday. For Christians, Easter is above all "the day that the Lord has made" (Ps. 118:24). The word *made* in verse 24 is frequently understood in terms of God's creative power, but it should also be heard as an affirmation of God's saving power. That is, "made" should be understood in the sense of effective activity. In fact, a better translation of verse 24*a* would be, "This is the day on which the Lord *has acted.*" God was active in the exodus; God was active in returning exiles; God was active in the life, death, and resurrection of Jesus. So the Gospel writers affirm in their use of Psalm 118. As a traditional call to worship, Psalm 118:24 is a reminder to Christians that every Sunday is a celebration of the resurrection, the Lord's Day, the day on which the Lord has acted and is still active.

THE PASSION OF JESUS: PSALMS 22, 31, AND 69

The influence of the Psalms upon the Gospel writers is clearest in the accounts of Jesus' suffering and death. Depending on how one counts them, thirteen to seventeen Old Testament texts are quoted or alluded to in the passion narratives. At least eight or nine of them are from Psalms 22, 31, and 69, all of which are prayers of persons who are suffering severely.[7] According to Luke, Jesus' final words from the cross are "Father, into your hands I commend my spirit" (23:46), a quotation of Psalm 31:5*a*. Thus Luke finally has Jesus claim the assurance contained in the Psalms, but only on the cross (compare Luke 4:9-11; see above). Psalm 69:4 is quoted by Jesus in John 15:25 to explain the hatred against him that has led to his suffering. In Mark 15:32, Jesus is taunted in a way that recalls Psalm 69:9; and the "wine mixed with myrrh" (Mark 15:32) and "sour wine" (Mark 15:36) offered to Jesus, are reminiscent of the psalmist's experience of being given "vinegar to drink" (Ps. 69:21).

But it is Psalm 22 that is most clearly reflected in the Passion accounts. According to Matthew and Mark, Jesus' only words from the cross are a quotation of the opening line of Psalm 22: "My God, my God, why have you forsaken me?" (Matt. 27:46; Mark 15:34). Furthermore, the details of the story are reminiscent of the psalmist's experience. Jesus is mocked by those who shake their heads at him (Matt. 27:39; Mark 15:29; Ps. 22:7), and the words of the mockers (Matt. 27:43) recall the words of those who mocked the psalmist (22:8). Jesus' thirst in John 19:28 recalls the psalmist's thirst (22:15), and Jesus' garments are divided as are the psalmist's (Matt. 27:35; Mark 15:24; Luke 23:34; John 19:24; Ps. 22:18).[8] Obviously, there is a relationship between Psalm 22 and the Gospel accounts. It should not be understood in terms of prediction and fulfillment. Rather, either Jesus intentionally embodied the experience of the faithful sufferer in Psalm 22, or the Gospel writers articulated their understanding of Jesus in the light of their knowledge of Psalm 22, or both. An examination of Psalm 22, entirely apart from its use in the New Testament, reveals why the psalm was such a rich theological resource for the Gospel writers' interpretation of Jesus.

The Shape, Content, and Message of Psalm 22

In many ways, Psalm 22 is like Psalms 3, 13, 88, and 130, the prayers discussed in chapter 5. It contains the elements of complaint and plea (vv. 1-21); it moves toward and ends in praise (vv. 22-31); it affirms God's presence in the depths. But while Psalm 22 may be typical in these ways, it is also unique; and commentators have recognized its particularity. Mays, for instance, suggests that Psalm 22 represents "a development of the type that raises it to its very limits and begins to transcend them."[9] And Ellen F. Davis speaks of the "balanced extravagances of the lament and the vow or call to praise."[10] According to Davis, it is the "poet's extravagance of expression" and "the exuberance of the poetic vision that *explodes the limits*" both of the typical form and "Israel's traditional understandings" of God and the world and of life and death.[11]

The psalmist's use of "the device of repetition or doubling" contributes to the intensity or extravagance of the complaint and the praise.[12] Both major sections of the psalm are composed of two smaller sections, giving the whole poem a sort of "double strength." The lament can be divided into verses 1-11 and 12-21. Verses 1-11 in turn consist of two complaints (vv. 1-2 and 6-8), each of which is followed by the psalmist's recalling of a better time, first for the whole people (vv. 3-5) and then for himself (vv. 9-10). As Davis suggests, the juxtaposition of the complaints and the recollections of past beneficence produces a "bitter irony"—while God is "enthroned on the praises of Israel" (v. 3), the psalmist grovels like a worm, scorned and despised by everyone (v. 6).[13] A concluding plea summarizes the sorry situation. God is "far" (v. 11; see "far" also in vv. 1 and 19); only "trouble is near."

The imagery shifts in verses 12-21 to provide a terrifying description of the trouble. Again, this section is composed of two complaints (vv. 12-13 and v. 16*ab*), each populated by animals that surround the psalmist (note the repetition of the Hebrew root *sbb*, "surround," in verses 12 and 16; the NRSV renders the two occurrences with "encircle" and "are all around"). Whereas the complaints in verses 1-11 were juxtaposed with recollections of better times, here each complaint is followed by a description that employs anatomical terms to indicate the nearness of death (vv. 14-15 and vv. 16*c*-18). The word *bones* is the first bodily part mentioned in verses 14-15 and the last mentioned in verses 16c-18, but also involved are the heart, breast, mouth, tongue, jaws, hands, and feet. The psalmist is in bad shape! Indeed, he can say to God that "you lay me in the dust of death" (v. 15), while his enemies can begin to appropriate his possessions (v. 18).

Like the first major section of the psalm, the second ends with a plea (vv. 19-21), which both reintroduces the cast of animal characters and provides a link to the first plea by way of the repetition of "far" and "help" (v. 19; see v. 11). The depth of the problem is indicated by the animal imagery that suggests that both the psalmist and his enemies have been utterly dehumanized, but something is changing. Whereas the psalmist had concluded that "there is no one to help" in verse 11, here he addresses God as "my help." This is the first clue that verses 19-21 are transitional. Further evidence is provided by the three verbs in verses 20-21—"deliver," "save," and "answer" (NRSV "rescued"). Each of these verbs occurs in one of the complaint sections of verses 1-11 with a negative sense. The enemies' taunts imply that God cannot "deliver" (v. 8; Hebrew *nzl*); and the psalmist complains that God is "so far from saving" (v. 1; NRSV, "helping," Hebrew *yš'*) and that God does "not answer" (v. 2). But the addressing of God as "my help," as well as the continuing plea for God to "deliver" and "save," indicates a remarkable depth of faith in an apparently hopeless, deathful situation. The final line of the lament is particularly important. The Hebrew should be translated literally as, "From the horns of the wild oxen you have answered me" (v. 21b). The opening complaint has been reversed! God has answered, but the answer comes not beyond the suffering but precisely *in the midst of and even from the suffering*. God is present in the depths and even in death (v. 15; see vv. 17-18).[14]

In a sense, the extravagant affirmation of verse 21b prepares for the praise section of the psalm (vv. 22-31), but the exuberance and extent of the praise are still surprising. In verses 22-26, the Hebrew root *hll*, "praise," occurs in every verse except the middle verse (v. 24), which gives the reasons for praise—God does "not despise or abhor the affliction of the afflicted." This reason sounds quite incredible in view of

verses 1-21, but something has changed! The affliction is still
very real, but the affliction itself has somehow become the
answer (see v. 21*b*). What the psalmist now affirms is that God
is present *in the affliction*. The praise he or she offers and invites
the congregation to offer (v. 23) comes out of the depths in the
midst of affliction. The four occurrences of *hll* in verses 22-26
recall verse 3, "enthroned on the praises of Israel," and remove
the "bitter irony" of that phrase. In verses 22-26, for God still
to be enthroned on Israel's praises must mean that God is
"enthroned" or "dwells" (the Hebrew can mean either one) in
the depths. In short, God is now positioned among the afflicted. God is not hiding God's face, and God can hear the
psalmist's cry (v. 24), because God is present. God does not
despise the affliction of the afflicted (v. 24). God shares it! The
forsakenness of the psalmist (v. 1) is the forsakenness of God.
If God is the source of the psalmist's death (v. 15), God is also
the source of the psalmist's praise (v. 25*a*). To praise God is to
live, and so verse 26*b* forms an appropriate conclusion to the
first unit of the praise section: "May your hearts live forever!"
In the face of the traditional Israelite understanding that death
constantly encroaches upon life, the psalmist affirms that life
encroaches upon death!

Traditional boundaries and borders are obliterated even
more completely in verses 27-31. The praise offered and the
testimony rendered in verses 22-26 have universal effects. "All
the ends of the earth" and "all the families of the nations" will
recognize God's rule (vv. 27-28). Ethnic and national boundaries are superseded; God's rule is extended in space and also
in time. Not only will "people yet unborn" (v. 31) recognize
God's rule, but even more remarkably, the dying and perhaps
those already dead will worship God as well (v. 29). To be sure,
the affirmation is not the traditional Israelite view of life and
death, and verse 29 is difficult to translate. The middle portion
of verse 29, however, is straightforward and is translated literally by the NRSV: "Before him shall bow all who go down to
the dust." That this phrase indicates death is even more likely
in view of verse 15, which mentions the "dust of death." Davis

summarizes well the meaning and significance of verse 29 and the entire section (vv. 27-31):

> It is likely that the psalm predates the time when the doctrine of an afterlife began to play a significant role in Jewish thought; for this there is clear evidence only in the Hellenistic period. . . . It seems, then, that the present invocation of the dead is much better explained in terms of the poet's extravagance of expression than in terms of the more sober development of religious dogma. Emerging suddenly out of a deathlike loss of meaning, the psalmist's joyful confidence that God is responsive to his plea demands that the dead above all may not be excluded from celebration and worship. It is the exuberance of the poetic vision that explodes the limits of Israel's traditional understandings. The shift in thought occurs first within the linguistic sphere, when a poet's productive imagination glimpses a possibility that only later (perhaps even centuries later) will receive doctrinal formulation as the resurrection of the dead.[15]

Psalm 22 and Jesus Christ

As Davis suggests, it is precisely this poetic explosion of limits that made Psalm 22 such a rich resource for the Gospel writers.[16] The psalm's new and expanded vision of God, of life, and of death informed the Gospel writers as they articulated what they had witnessed and experienced in Jesus of Nazareth. By telling the story of Jesus using Psalm 22, the Gospel writers affirm that in Jesus' faithful suffering, God was present and that God has opened up new possibilities for human life and death. They apparently saw in Psalm 22 a source for articulating the meaning of both the cross and the resurrection. Thus Jesus' cry from the cross (Mark 15:34; Matt. 27:46; Ps. 22:1) is not simply a cry of deriliction; it is also an affirmation of faith in a God who shares human affliction and who enables even the dead to offer God praise.

There is perhaps another dimension that made Psalm 22 so compelling for the Gospel writers. As Mays suggests, the psalm has an eschatological character; it affirms God's reign over all people and nations in all times and places. Elsewhere in the Old Testament God deals with peoples and nations through the whole people, Israel, or through a unique individual, the Davidic king (messiah). Thus Mays concludes concerning Psalm 22 in its original setting:

> Psalm 22 cannot be the prayer and praise of just any afflicted Israelite. Though we cannot know for certain for whom it was written and through what revisions it may have passed in the history of its use, in its present form the figure in the psalm shares in the corporate vocation of Israel and the messianic role of David.[17]

For the Gospel writers, who saw in Jesus the fulfillment of Israel's history and the arrival of the messiah, Psalm 22 thus represented an ideal resource. The effect of their use of Psalm 22 is in keeping with the central thrust of Jesus' proclamation, for as a commentary on Jesus' death and resurrection, Psalm 22 "interprets Jesus' passion and resurrection as a summons to the world (in the most inclusive sense of that term) to believe in the reign of the Lord."[18]

In essence, the Gospel writers recognized that Psalm 22 affirms what the story of Jesus affirms: God rules the world. Suffering and glory, cross and resurrection, are inseparable. The agony and the ecstacy belong together as the secret of our identity . . . and God's identity!

THE RESURRECTION AND THE FULLNESS OF TIME

As already suggested, Psalm 22 served the Gospel writers not only as they told the story of Jesus' death but also as they proclaimed Jesus' resurrection. But there is more to be said. The first recorded Christian sermon, Peter's sermon on the Day of Pentecost, is a proclamation of the resurrection; and the texts for the sermon are from the book of Psalms (Ps. 16:8-11 in Acts 2:24-28, 31; Ps. 132:11 in Acts 2:30; Ps. 110:1 in Acts 2:34-35). Psalms 110 and 132 are royal psalms; they deal with the Davidic king, the messiah, the Son of God, who was supposed both to embody God's rule and to represent the whole people. As such, Psalms 110 and 132 serve as testimonies for the New Testament writers who saw in Jesus the fulfillment of Israel's destiny and God's will for the institution of monarchy. For them, Jesus incarnated both authentic humanity and the divine will. Later in Acts, Peter cites Psalm 118:22 in proclaiming Jesus' resurrection; the rejected stone "has become the cornerstone" (Acts 4:11). As suggested above, it is still the practice of the church to use Psalm 118 on Easter, a tradition that probably originated very early.

In the broadest perspective, the New Testament writers cannot imagine the fullness of time without recourse to the psalms. In the Revelation to John, the "end of the world" will be accompanied by the singing of psalms. The twenty-four elders and the whole company of the faithful sing a "new song," an act reminiscent of Psalms 33:3; 96:1; and 98:1 (Rev. 5:9; 14:3). Later in the book, the faithful sing the Song of Moses and the Song of the Lamb, which is composed in part of quotations or allusions to Psalms 86:9-10 and 145:17 and the essential affirmation of which is the same as that of the Psalter—the Lord reigns (Rev. 15:3-4)!

Now, I am not a literalist nor an apocalypticist by any means. In fact, I think the world has been here for millions of years and will be here millions more, even if we human beings destroy ourselves in the meantime. In any case, the vision of Revelation is a refreshing contrast to the frightening scenarios of a nuclear holocaust or winter, or of a depleted ozone layer that allows the sun to fry us slowly to oblivion. In short, while I take very seriously the warnings of the scientists and philosophers, I prefer to trust that in the end, the faithful people of God—from here and there and yonder, from then and now and yet-to-come—will be gathered around the throne of God . . . singing a psalm!

APPENDIX

THE SINGING OF THE PSALMS

A BRIEF HISTORY

The Psalms were meant to be sung. With few exceptions, the Psalms were originally composed with the intention that they be experienced with music. There is ample evidence within the Psalms themselves of instrumental accompaniment, and there is corroboration from other ancient Near Eastern texts and visual art as to the techniques and importance of singing.[1] There is even some speculation that the Massoretic pointing of the Hebrew text is a clue to the degrees of the scale to which the Psalms were originally sung.[2]

Despite these indications and speculations, we cannot be sure how the Psalms were actually sung in the Temple or synagogues. We can find a hint from one of the earliest plain-song tones in the medieval church, the *Tonus Peregrinus*, which is strikingly similar to a tone used in medieval Jewish communities. Free chanting of the Psalms was apparently the common mode of expression in both Christian and Jewish communities of the early centuries A.D. and serves as a pointer toward the original musical context of the Psalms. The chant used in early Hebrew and Jewish worship was perhaps sung to a constant "sprung" rhythm, an effect replicated in the mid-twentieth century by Father Joseph Gelineau, as his response to the reforms of Vatican II, in an attempt to restore the congregational singing of the Psalms as originally intended (see list of resources below).

There is ample evidence that the Psalms were sung not only by a cantor or a priestly choir but also by congregations. Numerous psalms contain refrains that were undoubtedly used just as refrains are used in familiar hymnody today—as a way of involving everyone within the congregation at certain important points within the psalm. It is likely that Hebrew and Jewish congregations did not sing entire psalms, but participated primarily through the use of these refrains. The mysterious note "Selah" may have originated as a liturgical direction to signal congregational involvement.

The headings of many psalms also give musical direction to a choir or congregation, but again, their meaning is obscure.

Throughout the Middle Ages, the singing of Psalms in the church became increasingly the work of professional choirs of monks. With the early English Reformation, a new style of chant in harmony was devised, which also reached its truest expression in the voices of a skilled choir. These interpretations of the Psalms through choral plain song and Anglican chant nonetheless kept the singing of the Psalms away from the congregation. The Reformers of the sixteenth and seventeenth centuries sought to restore the Psalms to the congregation by setting them to well-known metrical tunes of the day. Congregations were now singing the entire psalm as had probably never been done in earlier times. At first the texts remained fairly true to the original psalm, and the rhythms were rather free. In the later Reformation, metres were further regularized and editions of the Psalter were produced that allowed the mixing and matching of various tunes and texts. Finally, in the eighteenth century, psalm paraphrases (in contrast to metered translations) became increasingly acceptable, as evidenced in the work of Isaac Watts and others. This permitted greater beauty of musical expression. Metrical psalmody undoubtedly contributed greatly to the knowledge and love of the book of Psalms by the worshiping body. The first book published in the New World was *The Bay Psalter*, testimony to the importance psalm-singing held in the lives of newcomers to America.

With the rise of spiritual songs and other hymnody of the nineteenth and twentieth centuries, the congregational singing of the Psalms declined (although many churches of the Reformed tradition continued exclusively singing the Psalms well into the twentieth century). By the middle of this century, the Psalms were primarily read in worship, sometimes in unison or responsively by the congregation. Although this mode of reading continued to permit some participation, the essential musical component of the Psalms was lost. Those psalms that continued to be sung in metrical form were often not recognized as psalms, and regarded as just yet more hymns of historical or contemporary composition.

During the last forty years of the twentieth century, there has been a revival in the singing of the Psalms within and by the congregation, as the truest expression of praise and prayer using the very language God and the people of God have given us. Many new arrangements of the Psalms have been written: metrical (hymn melodies), plain-chanted, responsorial, antiphonal, through-composed for cantor/choir and congregation, and more. Increasing numbers of churches are rediscovering the ancient treasures of psalm-singing.

INTRODUCING PSALM-SINGING IN THE LOCAL CHURCH

The Psalms were meant to be sung. The Directory for Worship of the Presbyterian Church (U.S.A.) puts it this way: "Psalms were created to be sung by the faithful as their response to God. Though they may be read responsively or in unison, their full power comes to expression when they are sung."[3] Congregations who have reintroduced the regular, intentional singing of the Psalms have experienced a renewal of vitality in worship and a deeper understanding of how God graciously speaks to us and how we might better respond in lives of praise.

Several steps may be taken to bring about this renewal:

1. Increase consciousness of the use of the Psalms in worship. Use as calls to worship, calls to confession, assurances of pardon, affirmations of faith, and so on. Always identify this use for what it is, so that the congregation will know that what they are hearing and speaking are the Psalms themselves. Include bulletin notes on the Psalms. Use frequently in preaching. Incorporate the lectionary psalm for each Sunday in the worship order in some way, most usually as a gradual (transitional lesson) from Old to New Testament lessons.

2. Read the Psalms responsively. If your congregation is accustomed to reading the Psalms as a responsive selection from your hymnal, vary the routine by having various portions (young/old, left/right, January-June/July-December birthdays, etc.) of the congregation read the alternating parts. Read the Psalms in unison. Read dramatically by assigning different parts to different readers.

3. Sing psalms from the hymnal. Identify the psalms that are in your hymnal and use them. Make sure to always acknowledge them *as psalms,* and not just as any other hymn.

4. Sing additional metrical paraphrases of psalms as inserts in your bulletin, sung to tunes familiar to your congregation. Fred Anderson's psalm paraphrases are especially well-phrased and easy to sing (see list of resources).

5. Introduce responsorial psalmody to your congregation.

Church musician and composer Hal H. Hopson offers these six steps:

> a) A reader and the congregation read the verses responsively with the choir interjecting a refrain after each pair of verses. The refrain should be a phrase from a well-known hymn. This first step gets the congregation accustomed to having a refrain as a part of the psalmody in the service.
>
> b) A reader and the choir read the verses responsively with everyone (the choir *and* congregation) singing the refrain after each pair of verses. Again, the refrain should be a phrase from a well-known hymn.
>
> c) A reader and the congregation read the verses responsively with the choir and congregation singing an antiphonal refrain [with the congregation simply repeating what the choir sings each time].
>
> d) A reader and the congregation read the verses responsively with the choir singing the refrain.
>
> e) A reader reads the verses; the choir and congregation sing the refrain.
>
> f) A cantor chants the verses on a simple tone with the choir and congregation singing the refrain.[4]

Some congregations will be able to skip quickly through these steps; others will need a very gradual introduction. It will be helpful to make clear in the bulletin and from the pulpit the reasons for and benefits from increased psalm-singing. Success is assured in any congregation if the pastor and/or church musician and choir are dedicated to this exciting task *and* if the introduction to psalm-singing is pursued with patience and persistence.

Be creative in your approach to the singing of the Psalms! Some congregations have found a fine reception when the children's choir does the leadership. Others respond well to their beloved pastors as cantors. Others appreciate the contributions of trained laypeople singing the Psalms or of a beautiful choir leading the congregation into song. Psalm-singing works well in large churches with many resources, or in very small churches where there is no choir. For further help, see "Training a Cantor" by Martha Hopson, and "Putting the Psalter to Work in a Congregation" by Sally Watkins Gant, in *Reformed Liturgy and Music* 26/2 (Spring 1992), pp. 78-83.[5]

RESOURCES

The following resources will prove helpful in singing the Psalms. A brief description is provided of most resources:

Anderson, Fred. *Singing Psalms of Joy and Praise*. Philadelphia: Westminster Press, 1986. Fifty-one excellent psalm paraphrases rendered metrically to be sung to familiar hymn tunes. Permission is granted to reproduce in church bulletins.

Chamberlain, Gary. *Psalms for Singing: 26 Psalms with Musical Settings for Congregation and Choir*. Nashville: The Upper Room, 1984. Responsorial arrangements using excellent translations by Chamberlain. Includes permission to copy congregational portions.

Daily Prayer. Philadelphia: Westminster Press, 1987. A few responsorial psalm arrangements are included for psalms in the daily office. Also chanting instructions and seasonal refrains.

Eslinger, Elise, ed. *The Upper Room Worshipbook*. Nashville: The Upper Room, 1985. A good psalm section.

Gelineau, Joseph. *The Gelineau Gradual*. Chicago: G.I.A. Publications, Inc., Edition G-2124. Arranged according to the lectionary.

———. *The Grail Gelineau Psalter*. Chicago: G.I.A. Publications, Inc. (No. G-1703). No antiphons, but includes metrical chants for *all* the psalms.

———. *20 Psalms and Three Canticles*. Chicago: G.I.A. Publications, Inc. (item # G-1476). There are also congregational books for this and the above two.

———. *24 Psalms and a Canticle*. Chicago: G.I.A. Publications, Inc. (item # G-1424). Note that Roman Catholic numbering of the Psalms differs by one in some cases from the Protestant tradition.

———. *30 Psalms and Two Canticles*. Chicago: G.I.A. Publications, Inc. (item # G-1430).

Haas, David, and Jeanne Cotter. *Celebration Series-Psalms for the Church Year*, vol. 3. Chicago: G.I.A. Publications, 1989.

Hallock, Peter. *The Ionian Psalter: Fifteen Psalms for the Seasons of the Church Year.* Mercer Island, Wash.: Ionian Arts, Inc., 1987 (PS801). Another fine collection of responsorial psalmody with congregational refrains included.

Haugen, Marty. *Celebration Series-Psalms for the Church Year*, vol. 2. Chicago: G.I.A. Publications, 1988 (No. G-3261). More of the above (parts of 15 psalms and three canticles). Also with permission to copy congregational refrains.

Haugen, Marty, and David Haas. *Celebration Series-Psalms for the Church Year.* G.I.A. Publications, 1983 (No. G-2664). Beautiful contemporary settings of 24 psalms. Permission to copy congregational refrains included.

Holbert, John, S. T. Kimbrough, Jr., and Carlton R. Young, eds. *Psalms for Praise and Worship: A Complete Liturgical Psalter.* Nashville: Abingdon Press, 1992. A wonderful new resource with translations *and* pointings for every psalm as well as 127 responses (largely familiar) with tones provided from *The Lutheran Book of Worship.* It is truly a complete Psalter.

Hopson, Hal H. *Eighteen Psalms.* Carol Stream, Ill.: Hope Publishing Co., 1990. Some duplication with *Psalm Refrains and Tones* (see below) but in an interlined format.

————. *Psalm Refrains and Tones for the Common Lectionary, with Inclusive Language for God and People.* Carol Stream, Ill.: Hope Publishing Co., 1988 (Code No. 425). The single most useful resource available. Responsorial arrangements for all psalm lections, with a familiar and an original refrain for each one. Verses from the NRSV or your favorite translation are pointed by you (instructions provided!) and sung to psalm tones included with each refrain. Permission is granted to copy refrains for congregational use.

————. *10 More Psalms.* Carol Stream, Ill.: Hope Publishing Co., 1990.

————. *10 Psalms.* Carol Stream, Ill.: Hope Publishing Co., 1986 (HH3930). A very valuable resource with permission to copy congregational refrains.

ICEL Lectionary Music: Psalms and Alleluia and Gospel Acclamations for the Liturgy of the Word. Chicago: G.I.A. Publications, 1982 (No. G-2626). Good arrangements that include permission to copy congregational inserts.

The Lutheran Book of Worship. Minneapolis: Augsburg, 1978. Includes a fine and traditional collection of lectionary psalms pointed for chanting to tones provided.

Marshall, Jane. *Psalms Together* and *Psalms Together II,* Choristers Guild (2834 W. Kingley Rd., Garland, Texas 75041). Distributed by The Lorenz Corporation, 501 E. Third St., Box 802, Dayton, Ohio 45401. Six unison antiphonal arrangements for choirs or cantor and congregation; all are small portions of psalms, but would be good for calls to worship, responses, and the like. The first volume includes permission to copy congregational refrains.

Melloh, John A., and William G. Storey. *Praise God in Song.* Chicago: G.I.A. Publications, 1979. An ecumenical daily prayer book with many psalm settings.

Music from Taizé, Responses, Litanies, Acclamations, Canons. Vols. 1 and 2. Chicago: G.I.A. Publications, 1981, 1984 (No. G-2433-P and G-2778-P). Some psalms are included in this famous music from the French monastic community.

The Presbyterian Hymnal: Hymns, Psalms, and Spiritual Songs. Philadelphia: Westminster, 1990. Includes an extensive section of metrical and some responsorial psalms.

Psalm Praise. Chicago: G.I.A. Publications, 1973. A good Roman Catholic resource with almost half the psalms represented, as well as traditional liturgical music and New Testament songs.

Psalms for the Cantor. Schiller Park, Ill.: World Library Publications, 1987. This series comes in seven volumes and follows the Roman Catholic lectionary. Permission to copy congregational inserts included.

The Psalter: Psalms and Canticles for Singing. Philadelphia: Westminster, 1993. An excellent resource containing a wide range of responsorial psalmody. Includes arrangements for all psalms in *The Revised Common Lectionary.* An effort has been made to include arrangements from many different traditions and in many styles. Contains congregational refrains with copyright permission for inclusion in church bulletins. An extremely valuable resource.

Psalter Hymnal. Grand Rapids: CRC Publications, 1988. From the Christian Reformed Church, this book includes all 150 psalms in metrical arrangement, plus hymns. No permission to copy.

Reformed Liturgy and Music. The Ministry Unit on Theology and Worship of the Presbyterian Church (U.S.A.), 1044 Alta Vista Rd., Louisville, Kentucky 40205. This periodical is excellent for psalm singers! Each issue includes suggestions for psalm settings for the psalms of the day for the upcoming section of *The Revised Common Lectionary,* as well as a good bibliography of psalm resources. Sometimes new psalm settings with permission to copy are included. Published quarterly. $15.00 per year.

Routley, Erik, ed. *Rejoice in the Lord.* Grand Rapids: Eerdmans, 1985. This fine hymnal of the Reformed Church in America has a good section of metrical psalms.

The United Methodist Hymnal. Nashville: The United Methodist Publishing House, 1989. Includes a large section of responsorial psalmody with congregational refrains and verses pointed for chanting or arranged for responsive reading.

NOTES

INTRODUCTION AND PURPOSE

1. John Calvin, *Commentary on the Book of Psalms,* vol. 1, (Edinburgh: Calvin Translation Society, 1845), p. xxxvi.

2. Martin Luther, "Preface to the Psalter" in *Luther's Works,* vol. 35 (Philadelphia: Fortress Press, 1960), pp. 255-56.

3. See Walter Brueggemann, "The Costly Loss of Lament," *JSOT* 36 (1986):57-71.

4. Rowland E. Prothero, *The Psalms in Human Life and Experience* (New York: E. P. Dutton and Co., 1903), p. 2.

5. Eugene H. Peterson, *Answering God: The Psalms as Tools for Prayer* (San Francisco: Harper & Row, 1989), p. 10; see also pp. 1-7.

6. Klaus Seybold, *Introducing the Psalms,* trans. R. G. Dunphy (Edinburgh: T. & T. Clark Ltd., 1990), p. 27; emphasis added. Seybold's view provides a necessary complement to Peterson's contention that the Psalms "are not provided to teach us about God but to train us in responding to him." See Peterson, *Answering God,* p. 12.

7. For a brief statement of this approach to the Psalms, see J. Clinton McCann, Jr., "The Psalms as Instruction," *Interpretation* 46 (1992):117-28. Material from this essay has been included in this introduction and in chapter 1 below and is used with the permission of the original publisher.

8. For a brief treatment in English, see Hermann Gunkel, *The Psalms: a Form-Critical Introduction,* trans. Thomas M. Horner (Philadelphia: Fortress Press, 1967). Gunkel's major types include hymn (song of praise), communal lament, lament of the individual, and thanksgiving song of the individual. Other types include entrance liturgies, torah songs, blessings, and royal psalms. For Gunkel's thorough treatment, see *Einleitung in die Psalmen: die Gattungen der religösen Lyrik Israels,* zu ende geführt von Joachim Begrich. 2nd ed. (Göttingen: Vandenhoeck und Ruprecht, 1966).

9. See Sigmund Mowinckel, *The Psalms in Israel's Worship,* trans. D. R. Ap-Thomas. 2 vols. (Nashville: Abingdon Press, 1962). The setting Mowinckel proposed for many of the psalms was an autumnal New Year Festival at which the enthronement of the Lord as king was celebrated and re-enacted. This influential hypothesis is no longer accepted by many scholars, since there is no direct biblical evidence for the existence of such a festival.

10. See, for instance, Claus Westermann, *Praise and Lament in the Psalms,* trans. Keith R. Crim and Richard N. Soulen (Atlanta: John Knox Press, 1981), pp. 15-35. Westermann introduced a distinction between declarative and descriptive praise. See also H. J. Kraus, *Psalms 1-59,* trans. H. C. Oswald (Minneapolis: Augsburg, 1988), pp. 38-62. Instead of identifying psalms by form or type, Kraus classifies according to what he calls a "theme-oriented form group," deriving the names for these groups from terms

that occur in the Hebrew Psalter. Erhard Gerstenberger has led the way in proposing new life-settings for the Psalms, especially in his attempt to relate the Psalms not only to large gatherings for public worship but also to rituals held by small groups such as the family or clan. See his *Psalms, Part 1, With an Introduction to Cultic Poetry*, vol. 14, Forms of the OT Literature (Grand Rapids: Eerdmans., 1988).

11. James Muilenburg, "Form Criticism and Beyond," *JBL* 88 (1969):1-18.
12. Ibid., p. 18.
13. Brevard Childs, "Reflections on the Modern Study of the Psalms." In *Magnalia Dei, The Mighty Acts of God: Essays in Memory of G. Ernest Wright*, eds. F. M. Cross, W. E. Lemke, P. D. Miller, Jr. (Garden City, N.Y.: Doubleday, 1976), p. 378.
14. Gerald H. Wilson, *The Editing of the Hebrew Psalter*, SBL Dissertation Series 76 (Chico, Calif.: Scholars Press, 1985). For a helpful summary of the scope and conclusions of the research on the shape and shaping of the Psalter, see David M. Howard, Jr., "Editorial Activity in the Psalter: A State-of-the-Field Survey," *Word and World* 9/3 (Summer 1989):274-85. This essay, accompanied by eight additional essays on the shape and shaping of the Psalter, has been reprinted in *The Shape and Shaping of the Psalter*, ed. J. Clinton McCann, Jr., JSOT Supplement Series 159 (Sheffield, England: JSOT Press, 1993).
15. See Wilson, *Editing*, pp. 204-7; Childs, *Introduction to the Old Testament as Scripture* (Philadelphia: Fortress Press, 1979), pp. 513-14. See also J. P. Brennan, "Psalms 1-8: Some Hidden Harmonies," *Biblical Theology Bulletin* 10 (1980); J. Rendl, "Weisheitliche Bearbeitung von Psalmen: Ein Beitrag zum Verständis der Sammlung des Psalter," *VTS* 32 (1981):333-56; G. T. Sheppard, *Wisdom as a Hermeneutical Construct: A Study in the Sapientializing of the OT* (New York: de Gruyter, 1980), pp. 136-43.
16. Childs, *Introduction*, p. 513.
17. James L. Mays, "The Place of the Torah-Psalms in the Psalter," *JBL* 106/1 (1987):3-12. Like other scholars, Mays treats Psalms 1, 19, and 119 as torah-psalms. He also finds expression of a similar theology in Psalms 18, 25, 33, 78, 89, 93, 94, 99, 103, 105, 111, 112, 147, 148; see p. 8.
18. Ibid., p. 12; italics added.
19. Childs, "Reflections," p. 385.
20. N. H. Ridderbos, "The Psalms: Style-Figures and Structure," *Oudtestamentische Studien* 13 (1963):44.
21. Calvin, *Commentary on the Book of Psalms*, pp. xxxviii-xxxix; italics added.
22. For an eloquent statement of the "world-making" power of liturgy, see Walter Brueggemann, *Israel's Praise: Doxology Against Idolatry and Ideology* (Philadelphia: Fortress Press, 1988), pp. 1-28, 157-60. Brueggemann concludes (p. 157) in part: "liturgy does indeed make a world."

1. THE PSALMS AS TORAH, THEN AND NOW

1. See James L. Mays, "The Place of the Torah-Psalms," *JBL* 106/1 (1987):3.: "In most introductory treatments, Psalms 1, 19, and 119 are among the leftovers." Many scholars begin with the laments; see Claus Westermann, *The Living Psalms*, trans. J. R. Porter (Grand Rapids: Eerdmans, 1989); and W. H. Bellinger, *Psalms: Reading and Studying the Book of Praises* (Peabody, Mass.: Hendrickson Publishers, 1990). Others begin with the songs of praise; see Bernhard W. Anderson, *Out of the Depths: The Psalms Speak for Us Today*, rev. ed. (Philadelphia: Westminster Press, 1983). All three of these treatments leave Psalm 1 until last. In contrast, James Limburg does begin at the beginning in his *Psalms for Sojourners* (Minneapolis: Augsburg, 1986).

2. G. T. Rothuizen, *Landscape: a Bundle of Thoughts About the Psalms (the first fifty)*, trans. J. F. Jansen (Richmond: John Knox Press, 1965), p. 12. Rothuizen goes on to characterize this as "a wrong view."

3. See F. Brown, S. R. Driver, C. A. Briggs, *Hebrew and English Lexicon of the Old Testament* (Oxford: Clarendon Press, 1968), pp. 435-36.

4. See Gerald Wilson, *The Editing of the Hebrew Psalter*, SBL Dissertation Series 76 (Chico, Calif.: Scholars Press, 1985), pp. 139-67. Wilson has demonstrated that the five-book arrangement is not merely coincidental as some scholars have claimed.

5. See, for instance, Arthur Weiser, *The Psalms*, Old Testament Library, trans. Herbert Hartwell (Philadelphia: Westminster Press, 1962), pp. 197-204; H. J. Kraus, *Psalms 1-59*, trans. H. C. Oswald (Minneapolis: Augsburg, 1988), pp. 267-76.

6. See Mays, "Place of the Torah-Psalms," p. 5.

7. Leopold Sabourin, *The Psalms: Their Origin and Meaning* (New York: Alba House, 1974), p. 381.

8. Claus Westermann, *The Psalms: Structure, Content, and Message*, trans. Ralph D. Gehrke (Minneapolis: Augsburg, 1980), p. 117; italics added.

9. This suggestion has been made by Claus Westermann in *Praise and Lament in the Psalms*, trans. Keith R. Crim and Richard N. Soulen (Atlanta: John Knox Press, 1981), p. 253. Westermann reflects the opinion of the majority of scholars that the Psalter reached its present form by way of a process of collection and editing.

10. Wilson, *Editing*, pp. 222-28.

11. Mays, "Place of the Torah-Psalms," p. 8. Mays identifies other psalms with *torah* as a theme as follows: Psalms 18, 25, 33, 78, 89, 93, 94, 99, 103, 105, 111, 112, 147, 148.

12. See Robert Alter, *The Art of Biblical Poetry* (New York: Basic Books, Inc., 1985), pp. 114-17.

13. Patricia Blake, "Game Plan," *Time* 131/25, June 20, 1988, p. 86; italics added.

14. Ibid.

15. For a brief account of Sharansky's ordeal and the role of the Psalms, see Suzanne F. Singer, "The Power of the Psalms in Our Time," *Bible Review* 2/3 (Fall 1986):4. See also James Limburg, "Martin Luther and Natan Sharansky on the Same Seminary Program," *Bible Review* 4/4 (August 1988):10-11. For a full account, see Natan Sharansky, *Fear No Evil*, trans. Stefani Hoffman (New York: Random House, 1988).

16. Tom Long, oral presentation on the "Holy Week Scriptures, Year B," Montreat Conference on Music and Worship, Montreat, North Carolina, June 24, 1987.

17. James L. Mays, commenting on Psalm 1 in *The Book of Psalms*, Interpretation (Philadelphia: John Knox/Westminster, forthcoming).

18. Gary Chamberlain, *The Psalms: A New Translation for Prayer and Worship* (Nashville: The Upper Room, 1984), p. 26.

19. Flannery O'Connor, *The Complete Stories* (New York: Farron, Straus, and Giroux, 1971), pp. 131-33.

20. Walker Percy, *Lost in the Cosmos: The Last Self-Help Book* (New York: Washington Square Press, 1983), p. 12.

21. Richard Osmer, *A Teachable Spirit: Recovering the Teaching Office in the Church* (Louisville: Westminster/John Knox Press, 1990), p. 13; see also pp. 46-58. As Osmer points out, Calvin describes his conversion as God's having "brought my mind to a teachable frame" (p. 52). Interestingly, Calvin relates this to his readers in his Preface to his *Commentary on the Book of Psalms*.

2. THE PSALMS AND THE REIGN OF GOD

1. See J. P. Brennan, "Psalms 1-8: Some Hidden Harmonies," *Biblical Theology Bulletin* 10 (1980):25-26, who calls attention to these links.

2. See Gunkel, *The Psalms: A Form-Critical Introduction*, trans. Thomas M. Horner (Philadelphia: Fortress Press, 1967), pp. 23-24, as well as the standard form-critical commentaries.

3. James L. Mays, comment on Psalm 2 in *The Book of Psalms*, Interpretation (Louisville: Westminster/John Knox, forthcoming). I am also indebted to my colleague Deborah Krause for insights concerning the interpretation of Psalm 2.

4. Gerald H. Wilson, *The Editing of the Hebrew Psalter*, SBL Dissertation Series 76 (Chico, Calif.: Scholars Press, 1985), p. 212; see also pp. 209-14. See also Wilson, "The Use of the Royal Psalms at the 'Seams' of the Hebrew Psalter," *JSOT* 35 (1986): 88-92.

5. Ibid., pp. 213-14.

6. Ibid., p. 215.

7. See Sigmund Mowinckel, *The Psalms in Israel's Worship*, trans. D. R. Ap-Thomas, 2 vols. (Nashville: Abingdon Press, 1962), pp. 106-92.

8. Wilson, "The Use of the Royal Psalms," p. 92.

9. James L. Mays, "The Place of the Torah-Psalms in the Psalter," *JBL* 106/1 (1987):10. It is interesting that form critic Erhard Gersternberger also now suggests that Psalm 2 functioned eschatologically in the post-exilic era; see *Psalms, Part 1, with an Introduction to Cultic Poetry*, vol. 14 Forms of the OT Literature (Grand Rapids: Eerdmans, 1988), pp. 44-50.

10. See Terence Collins, "Decoding the Psalms: A Structural Approach to the Psalter" *JSOT* 37 (1987):41-60. By means of a very different approach, Collins arrives at conclusions very similar to mine; that is, the Psalter is didactic and eschatological in orientation. In particular, the "binary oppositions of people, ways and results" (p. 49) in Psalm 1 (as well as in Psalm 2, in my view) function to "call for a decision" (p. 50).

11. I am indebted to the following students at Eden Seminary for their insight about Psalm 95: David Gerth, Lucinda Hunter, and Karalee Mulkey.

12. Cited in Henri J. M. Nouwen, *The Wounded Healer* (Garden City, N.Y.: Image Books, 1972), pp. 94-95; see pp. 81-82. The story is taken from the tractate Sanhedrin.

13. Mays, "Place of the Torah-Psalms," p. 10; see James L. Mays, "The David of the Psalms," *Interpretation* 40 (1986):155, where, on the basis of an analysis of "The David of the Psalms," Mays concludes: "The relation of the Psalms to David brings out and emphasizes the organizing, unifying subject of the Psalter, namely, the Kingdom of God."

14. Flannery O'Connor, *The Complete Stories* (New York: Farrar, Straus, and Giroux, 1971), pp. 486-87.

3. PRAISE AND IDENTITY: THE MAJESTY OF GOD AND THE GLORY OF MORTALS

1. See Claus Westermann, *The Psalms: Structure, Content and Message*, trans. Ralph D. Gehrke (Minneapolis: Augsburg, 1980), pp. 59-60, where he describes the structure of the individual lament. As he points out (p. 60), "In their concluding parts a great number of IL [individual lament] psalms turn into words of praise to God."

2. Claus Westermann, *Praise and Lament in the Psalms*, trans. Keith R. Crim and Richard N. Soulen (Atlanta: John Knox Press, 1981), p. 257.

3. Ibid., p. 155.

4. Ibid., pp. 160-61.

5. Patrick D. Miller, Jr., *Interpreting the Psalms* (Philadelphia: Fortress Press, 1986), p. 70.

6. From the album cover of Duke Ellington's *Sacred Sounds*, The Prestige Series, P-24045. My thanks to James Limburg, who called this to my attention; see his *Psalms for Sojourners* (Minneapolis: Augsburg, 1986), pp. 91-92.

7. AP photo in *The St. Louis Post-Dispatch*, February 12, 1990, Section B, p. 1.

8. Walker Percy, *Lost in the Cosmos: The Last Self-Help Book* (New York: Washington Square Press, 1983), p. 178.

9. The words *ḥesed* and *ʾemet* occur frequently in the Psalms as a pair, thus providing regular recollections of Exodus 34:6; see 25:10; 40:10, 11; 57:3; 61:7; 85:10; 86:15; 89:14; 115:1; 138:2. In several additional cases, the words are not precisely paired but occur in the same verse, as in 117:2—see 26:3; 57:10; 69:13; 108:4. Also, *ḥesed* occurs several times with a similar word for "faithfulness" (*ʾemûnâ*, from the root *ʾmn*, from which *ʾ* is also derived) in Pss. 88:11; 89:2, 24; 92:2; 98:3; 100:5. Apart from its relationship to the root *ʾmn*, *ḥesed* is a key word, occuring in nearly a third of the Psalms. As subsequent discussions will point out, God's "steadfast love" is celebrated in Israel's songs of praise (see Pss. 48:9; 100:5; 118:1-4, 29); it is appealed to in Israel's prayers (see Pss. 13:5; 32:10; 51:1; 90:14; 109:21, 26); it is a vital component of Israel's professions of faith (see Ps. 23:6). For a thorough study of the word *ḥesed*, see Katharine Doob Sakenfeld, *Faithfulness in Action: Loyalty in Biblical Perspective*, Overtures to Biblical Theology (Philadelphia: Fortress Press, 1985), pp. 83-100 deal with *ḥesed* in the Psalms.

10. Walter Brueggemann, *The Message of the Psalms* (Minneapolis: Augsburg Press, 1984), pp. 37-38.

11. Robert Alter, *The Art of Biblical Poetry* (New York: Basic Books, 1985), p. 119.

12. Quoted in Tom Uhlenbrock, "Experts Say Earth Nearing Its Capacity," *The St. Louis Post-Dispatch*, October 27, 1990, Section A, p. 1. For an interpretation of Psalm 8 that focuses on ecological concerns, see James Limburg, "Who Cares for the Earth? Psalm 8 and the Environment," *Word and World* Supplement Series 1 (1992): 43-52. See also James L. Mays, " 'What is Man . . ?' Reflections on Psalm 8" in *From Faith to Faith: Essays in Honor of Donald G. Miller on his 70th Birthday*, ed. D. Y. Hadidian (Pittsburgh: Pickwick Press, 1979), pp. 203-18.

13. Westermann, *Praise and Lament*, p. 161.

14. "On the Edge of Heaven," *St. Louis Post-Dispatch*, September 20, 1987.

15. The Hebrew word *kābôd* underlies the NRSV's "honor" in Psalm 4:2 and "glory" in Psalm 8:5.

16. See, for instance, Job 3, Job's opening soliloquy cursing the day of his birth. Note especially the recurring image of light and darkness, day and night in relation to Genesis 1. See J. Gerald Janzen, *Job*, Interpretation (Atlanta: John Knox, 1985), pp. 61-71.

17. Janzen highlights the importance of Psalm 8 for the book of Job; see ibid., pp. 81-83, 174-77, 229-30, 245-46, 254-59.

18. Ibid., pp. 254-56.

19. Ibid., pp. 257-58.

20. Genesis 1:27; the phrase does not occur in Psalm 8 nor the book of Job, but the content of both texts suggests the same understanding of human identity that is present in Genesis 1.

21. Janzen, *Job*, pp. 258-59; see pp. 246-47.

22. See Brevard Childs, *Biblical Theology in Crisis* (Philadelphia: Westminster Press, 1970), pp. 160-63.

23. James L. Mays, "Worship, World, and Power," *Interpretation* 23 (1969):316. Mays cites A. F. Kirkpatrick, *The Book of Psalms* (Cambridge: Cambridge University Press, 1912), pp. 587-88.

24. Rowland E. Prothero, *The Psalms in Human Life and Experience* (New York: E. P. Dutton and Co., 1903), p. 114.

25. Mays, "Worship, World, and Power," p. 321. See Pss. 2:11; 18:43; 22:30; 72:11; 97:7; 102:22.

26. Ibid., p. 319. The "recognition formula" occurs frequently in Ezekiel.

27. Mays prefers the latter, citing other texts where "make" refers to the election and saving of Israel: Psalm 95:6-7; Deuteronomy 32:6, 15; Isaiah 43:1, 21; 44:2. See ibid., p. 324. Brueggemann understands "make" as a reference to creation; see his "Psalm 100," *Interpretation* 39 (1985):67.

28. Westermann, *Praise and Lament*, p. 161.

29. Brueggemann, "Psalm 100," p. 69.

30. Ibid., p. 69; see also Geoffrey Wainwright, *Doxology* (New York: Oxford University Press, 1980), p. 425.

31. Percy, *Lost in the Cosmos*, p. 141.

32. Ibid., p. 156.

33. Ibid.

34. Ibid.

35. The translation is that of Gary Chamberlain, *The Psalms: A New Translation for Prayer and Worship* (Nashville: The Upper Room, 1984), p. 26.

36. Percy, *Lost in the Cosmos*, pp. 156-57.

37. Flannery O'Connor, *The Complete Stories* (New York: Farrar, Straus, and Giroux, 1971), p. 492.

38. Ibid., p. 507.

39. Ibid., pp. 508-9.

4. PRAISE AND ACTIVITY: WHO SHALL ASCEND THE HILL OF THE LORD?

1. See, for instance, Erhard Gerstenberger, *Psalms, Part 1, With an Introduction to Cultic Poetry*, vol. 14, Forms of the OT Literature (Grand Rapids: Eerdmans, 1988), p. 118.

2. H. J. Kraus, *Psalms 1-59*, trans. H. C. Oswald (Minneapolis: Augsburg, 1988), p. 312.

3. See Sigmund Mowinckel, *The Psalms in Israel's Worship*, trans. D. R. Ap-Thomas, 2 vols. (Nashville: Abingdon Press, 1962), vol. 1, pp. 142, 170, 172. Weiser even proposes that Psalm 24 would have represented the climax of this festival; see Arthur Weiser, *The Psalms*, Old Testament Library, trans. Herbert Hartwell (Philadelphia: Westminster Press, 1962), p. 232.

4. Gerstenberger, *Psalms, Part 1*, p. 119. Gerstenberger also reviews briefly the several other proposals.

5. R. A. F. Mackenzie, *The Psalms—a Selection*, Old Testament Reading Guide 23 (Collegeville, Minn.: The Liturgical Press, 1967), p. 41.

6. William H. Willimon and Stanley Hauerwas, *Resident Aliens: Life in the Christian Colony* (Nashville: Abingdon Press, 1989), pp. 88, 90.

7. Ibid., p. 48.

8. Ibid., pp. 69-92.

9. Ibid., p. 90.

10. Jack Kingsbury, "The Place, Structure, and Meaning of the Sermon on the Mount Within Matthew," *Interpretation* 42 (1987):143.

11. Peter Craigie, "Psalm 113," *Interpretation* 39 (1985):70.

12. Willimon and Hauerwas, *Resident Aliens*, p. 36.

13. Reinhold Niebuhr, *Leaves from the Notebook of a Tamed Cynic* (San Francisco: Harper & Row, 1980), p. 147.

14. Flannery O'Connor, *The Complete Stories* (New York: Farrar, Straus, and Giroux, 1971), p. 454.

15. Ibid., p. 474.

16. Ibid., p. 480.

17. Donald W. McCullough, "God of My Cause," *The Presbyterian Outlook*, 172/36, October 22, 1990, p. 9.

18. Willimon and Hauerwas, *Resident Aliens*, pp. 36-37; italics added.

5. PRAYER AND IDENTITY: OUT OF THE DEPTHS

1. *The Hymnbook* (Richmond, N.Y., and Philadelphia: Presbyterian Church in the U.S.; United Presbytrian Church in the U.S.A.; Reformed Church of America, 1955). The book also includes fourteen other psalms that are customarily classified neither as praise/thanksgiving nor lament psalms. According to the classification of Leopold Sabourin, there are 41 psalms of praise/thanksgiving in the Psalter and 56 laments; see Sabourin, *The Psalms* (New York: Alba House, 1974), p. 443.

2. Walter Brueggemann, *The Message of the Psalms* (Minneapolis: Augsburg Press, 1984), p. 52.

3. Walter Brueggemann, "The Costly Loss of Lament," *JSOT* 36 (1986):61-65.

4. In his contemporary typology of the psalms, Brueggemann includes the lament in his "Psalms of Disorientation"; see *Message of the Psalms*, pp. 15-23, 51-122. See his treatment of Psalm 130, pp. 104-6, as well as that of Patrick D. Miller, Jr., *Interpreting the Psalms* (Philadelphia: Fortress Press, 1986), pp. 138-43.

5. It is, perhaps, helpful to think in terms of varying intensifications of God's presence; see Terence Fretheim, *The Suffering of God* (Philadelphia: Fortress Press, 1984), pp. 60-78. As Fretheim suggests, "The Old Testament language of absence (e.g. 'hide', 'withdraw', 'forsake', etc.) always entails presence at some level of intensification, albeit diminished" (p. 65).

6. Rowland E. Prothero, *The Psalms in Human Life and Experience* (New York: E. P. Dutton and Co., 1903), p. 141.

7. Ibid., p. 230.

8. See Brevard Childs, *Introduction to the Old Testament as Scripture* (Philadelphia: Fortress Press, 1979), pp. 521-22.

9. Klaus Seybold, *Introducing the Psalms*, trans. R. G. Dunphy (Edinburgh: T. & T. Clark Ltd., 1990), p. 127, points out that Psalm 3 initiates a series (Psalms 3–10) in which, with the possible exception of Psalm 8, the psalmist "knows the oppression of hostile powers." The whole series, like the final verse of Psalm 2, "traces in many aspects and variants the shared attitude which is expressed in the verb *hsh*, 'trust', 'have faith': taking refuge under the protection of the gracious God."

10. William H. Willimon and Stanley Hauerwas, *Resident Aliens: Life in the Christian Colony* (Nashville: Abingdon Press, 1989), p. 36.

11. James L. Mays, *The Book of Psalms*, Interpretation (Philadelphia: John Knox/Westminster, forthcoming).

12. Robert Alter, *The Art of Biblical Poetry* (New York: Basic Books, 1985), p. 65.

13. For a helpful review of the proposals, see Miller, *Interpreting the Psalms*, pp. 4-8; for Psalm 13 in particular, see Erhard Gerstenberger *Psalms, Part 1, With an Introduction to Cultic Poetry*, vol. 14, Forms of the OT Literature (Grand Rapids: Eerdmans, 1988),pp. 83-86.

14. Miller, *Interpreting the Psalms*, p. 8; see pp. 48-52.

15. Walter Brueggemann, *Praying the Psalms* (Winona, Minn.: St. Mary's Press, 1988), p. 31. See also Richard N. Boyce, *The Cry to God in the Old Testament*, SBL Dissertation Series 103 (Atlanta: Scholars Press, 1988). On the basis of a comprehensive study of the Hebrew roots z'q/ṣ'q, Boyce concludes that biblical prayer is fundamentally petitionary; see especially pp. 2-3, 71-73.

16. See Miller, *Interpreting the Psalms*, pp. 48-49; Claus Westermann, *The Living Psalms*, trans. J. R. Porter (Grand Rapids: Eerdmans, 1989), pp. 69-70.

17. M. Douglas Meeks, *God the Economist: The Doctrine of God and Political Economy* (Minneapolis: Fortress Press, 1989), p. 18.

18. For more, see William F. Woo, "War's Aftermath: Children Dying," *The St. Louis Post Dispatch*, May 26, 1991, p. B1. The remarks of comedian A. Whitney Brown are both humorous and scary. He suggests we have reached the limits of the "smart bomb" technology, for if they get any smarter, they'll refuse to go to war.

19. Lance Marrow, "Evil," *Time* 137/23, June 10, 1991, p. 49.

20. James L. Mays, "A Question of Identity: The Three-fold Hermeneutic of Psalmody," lecture delivered at Eden Theological Seminary, April 2, 1991.

21. See Seybold, *Introducing the Psalms*, pp. 39-43, who suggests this kind of prayer was written after a petition had been made and the prayer answered. He also theorizes that such "personal testimony in the form of a scroll" could be offered in the Temple in place of sacrifice. In his view, this practice accounts for the origin of the complaint or lament psalms. He concludes (p. 42): "Since the petition for help in time of crisis was the best documentation of the experience of prayer being answered, it seems to have become the custom to present this along with the 'new song'. This makes some of the many lament-praise combinations more easily understandable (e.g. Pss. 22; 30; 41; 69; etc.) and it also helps explain why prayers spoken in lonely times of need were recorded and passed down. To write them down was to testify they had been answered." See also Brueggemann, *Message of the Psalms*, pp. 59-60.

22. For this view or variations of it, see Gerstenberger, *Psalms, Part 1*, p. 85; Westermann, *The Living Psalms*, p. 74.

23. James L. Mays, "Psalm 13," *Interpretation* 34 (1980):281-82.

24. For a clear and helpful treatment of how Paul holds cross and resurrection together, see Charles B. Cousar, *A Theology of the Cross: The Death of Jesus in the Pauline Letters*, Overtures to Biblical Theology (Minneapolis: Fortress Press, 1990), pp. 88-108. Cousar also points out how Paul's theology of cross and resurrection shapes the Christian life. In his discussion of Philippians 3:2-11, Cousar concludes (p. 161): "Instead of discovering that sufferings may be endured for a time because the sufferers ultimately will be vindicated, we find in the text that the resurrection-power comes to expression in the very midst of tribulations."

25. Peter De Vries, *The Blood of the Lamb* (New York: Penguin Books, 1961), p. 52.

26. This characteristic movement occurs in several ways and has been variously labeled by form critics—"certainty of being heard," "assurance of being heard," "vow to praise," "words of praise," "confession of trust," etc. See, for instance, Westermann, *Praise and Lament in the Psalms*, trans. Keith R. Crim and Richard N. Soulen (Atlanta: John Knox Press, 1981), pp. 64-71.

27. The final phrase of the psalm is difficult to translate. It reads literally "my companions dark place." The NRSV supplies a preposition and a form of the verb *to be*: "my companions are in darkness." An alternative is to supply a form of the verb *to be* and accept a disagreement between subject and predicate nominative or perhaps

understand "my companions" collectively; "my company (is) darkness." The Grail translation reads, "my one companion is darkness," which fits the context of the psalm much better. See *The Psalms: An Inclusive Language Version Based on the Grail Translation from the Hebrew* (Chicago: G.I.A. Publications, 1983), p. 127.

28. Brueggemann, *Message of the Psalms*, pp. 78, 81.

29. Jesus' cry from the cross is a quotation from Psalm 22, another prayer of lament. Psalm 22 has much more evidently shaped the Gospel accounts of Jesus' passion than any other psalm (see the conclusion); however, other lament psalms inform the passion narrative, including Psalms 31 and 69, and it seems to me, Psalm 88. Interestingly, the relatively infrequent Hebrew word for "companions" occurs also in Psalm 31:11 (NRSV, "acquaintances"), a psalm Jesus quotes from the cross in Luke's account (Luke 23:46; Ps. 31:5).

30. William Styron, *Sophie's Choice* (Toronto: Bantam Books, 1979), pp. 614-15. Brueggemann calls attention to Styron's use of Psalm 88; see *Message of the Psalms*, p. 81.

6. PRAYER AND IDENTITY: FOR I KNOW MY TRANSGRESSIONS

1. The Penitential Psalms are as follows: 6, 32, 38, 51, 102, 130, 143. They constitute not a form critical grouping but rather an ecclesiastical grouping. For centuries, perhaps as early as Augustine, the church has considered these seven psalms as a group; and the Pentential Psalms have occupied a special place in the church's life.

2. I am indebted to the following students at Eden Seminary for insight about Psalm 51: Carol DeVaughan, Kathleen Kahl, Deborah Patterson, Danny Roman, Beth Tanner.

3. Concerning the relationship of Psalm 51 to David, see Michael Goulder, *The Prayers of David (Psalms 51-72): Studies in the Psalter, II*, JSOT Supplement Series (JSOT SS) 102 (Sheffield, England: JSOT Press, 1990). Goulder goes well beyond my view that the superscription provides a narrative context for hearing Psalm 51. He suggests that the superscription is historically accurate, that Psalm 51 was written shortly after David's murder of Uriah, and furthermore, that Psalms 51-72 are in chronological order and are David's response to the events narrated in 2 Samuel 11-1 Kings 2. See especially Goulder's statement of his hypothesis (pp. 24-30) and his exegesis of Psalm 51 (pp. 51-69).

4. A. Whitney Brown, *The Big Picture: An American Commentary* (New York: Harper Perennial, 1991), p. 12.

5. See Claus Westermann, *Elements of OT Theology*, trans. D. W. Stott (Atlanta: John Knox Press, 1982), p. 50.

6. See also Luke 24:44-49, where the disciples are commissioned to proclaim "repentance and forgiveness of sins" when they receive "power from on high." In John 21:15-19, Peter is forgiven and given a special mission to perform.

7. After Paul writes to the Corinthians of the "new creation" and his "ministry of reconciliation" among them (2 Cor. 5:16-21), he reveals what the preaching of grace involves—every manner of affliction (2 Cor. 6:4-5). Jesus too, of course, experienced the violent reaction of those who were scandalized by his readiness to extend the grace of God to sinners.

8. See, for instance, H. J. Kraus, *Psalms 1-59*, trans. H. C. Oswald (Minneapolis: Augsburg, 1988), p. 506.

9. I am indebted to former Eden student Julia Allen Berger for insights about Psalm 32.

10. Robert Jenson, "Psalm 32," *Interpretation* 33 (1979):175.

11. Rowland E. Prothero, *The Psalms in Human Life and Experience* (New York: E. P. Dutton and Co., 1903), p. 29.

7. PRAYER AND ACTIVITY: VENGEANCE, CATHARSIS, AND COMPASSION

1. Walter Brueggemann, *The Message of the Psalms* (Minneapolis: Augsburg Press, 1984), p. 83. See also Brueggemann, "Psalm 109: Three Times 'Steadfast Love,' " *Word and World* 5 (1985):144-54.

2. It should be noted that even when one opts for the procedure followed by the NRSV, one still must deal with the issue of the psalmist's desire for vengeance. In verse 20, the psalmist claims the "song of hate" as an expression of his or her own desire for the accusers: "May that [RSV, "this"; that is, the curses of vv. 8-19] be the reward of my accusers from the LORD" (NRSV).

3. Stan Berenstain and Jan Berenstain, *The Berenstain Bears and the In-Crowd* (New York: Random House, 1989).

4. Walter Brueggemann, *Praying the Psalms* (Winona, Minn.: St. Mary's Press, 1988), p. 68.

5. C. S. Lewis, *Reflections on the Psalms* (New York: Harcourt, Brace and Co., 1958), p. 24.

6. See Brueggemann, *Message of the Psalms,* pp. 85-88.

7. As explained in note 2 above, I am assuming the psalmist is speaking in verse 6; however, in the NRSV, the relationship between verses 6 and 31 is even more striking. Whereas the enemy wishes for an accuser to stand at the psalmist's right (v. 6), the psalmist affirms that it is God who "stands at the right hand of the needy" (v. 31).

8. James L. Mays, "A Question of Identity: The Three-fold Hermeneutic of Psalmody," lecture delivered at Eden Theological Seminary, April 2, 1991.

9. Quoted in Judith Newark, "Elie Wiesel and the Two Who Saved His Life," *The St. Louis Post Dispatch,* October 5, 1988, p. E6.

10. Ewald Bach, "By the Babylonian Rivers" in *The Hymnal of the United Church of Christ* (Philadelphia: United Church Press, 1974); no. 257.

11. Frederick Buechner, *Whistling in the Dark* (San Francisco.: Harper & Row, 1988), p. 100.

12. Patrick D. Miller, Jr., *Interpreting the Psalms* (Philadelphia: Fortress Press, 1986), p. 120.

13. See ibid., p. 124, who concludes: "Justice is the issue on which the very claims of deity are settled. Justice, just rule, is that central activity by which God is God. Without it the very universe cannot survive." On the importance of verse 5 as the central verse of Psalm 82, see L. K. Handy, "Sounds, Words and Meanings in Psalm 82," *JSOT* 47 (1990):51-66.

8. ASSURANCE: YOU ARE WITH ME

1. Walter Brueggemann, *The Message of the Psalms* (Minneapolis: Augsburg Press, 1984), p. 154.

2. See above, chap. 3, and chap. 5.

3. Brueggemann, *The Message of the Psalms,* pp. 154-55.

4. H. J. Kraus, *Psalms 1-59,* trans. H. C. Oswald (Minneapolis: Augsburg, 1988), p. 308.

5. See, for instance, Patrick D. Miller, Jr., *Interpreting the Psalms* (Philadelphia: Fortress Press, 1986), p. 117, who suggests that the possible reference to the Temple and the mention of "a table" in verse 5 may indicate "that the psalm had an original setting in practices of worship, more specifically, the occasion of a thanksgiving meal

offered by a person in gratitude to God and fulfillment of vows made in seeking God's help." Mannati includes Psalm 23 (along with Psalms 4, 5, 16, 31, 36, 49, 63, 73, 139) in a category he calls "psalms of the guest of Yahweh," the dramatic performance of which included a representative of the people spending the night in the Temple in order to receive an oracle of assurance of the people's chosenness; see M. Mannati, *Les Psaumes 1* (E. de Solms: Desclée de Brouwer, 1966), pp. 51-53. Psalm 23 has traditionally been categorized as a "psalm of confidence" or a "psalm of trust"; see Leopold Sabourin, *The Psalms* (New York: Alba House, 1974), pp. 270-73. For a summary of proposed settings, see Kraus, *Psalms 1-59*, pp. 305-6. For similar passages in the Psalms, see 27:4-6; 36:7-9; 52:8-9; 61:4.

6. Erhard Gerstenberger, *Psalms, Part 1, With an Introduction to Cultic Poetry*, vol. 14, Forms of the OT Literature (Grand Rapids: Eerdmans, 1988), p. 115.

7. I am indebted to my colleague John Bracke for insight into the possible relationship between Psalms 22 and 23; see also Miller, *Interpreting the Psalms*, p. 118.

8. Isaac Watts, 1719, altered 1972 in *Hymns, Psalms, and Spiritual Songs* (Louisville: Westminster/John Knox, 1990), no. 172.

9. Tillie Olsen, *Tell Me a Riddle* (New York: Dell Publishing, 1961), pp. 33-34.

10. Ibid., p. 51.

11. M. Douglas Meeks, *God the Economist: The Doctrine of God and Political Economy* (Minneapolis: Fortress Press, 1989), p. 180.

12. Ibid., p. 180; italics added.

13. Klaus Seybold, *Introducing the Psalms*, trans. R. G. Dunphy (Edinburgh: T. & T. Clark Ltd., 1990), p. 127; italics added.

14. Psalm 46 is traditionally categorized as a Zion Song or Hymn to Zion along with Psalms 48, 76, 84, 87, and 122. See chapter 9 for a further consideration of the significance of holy space. For a good summary of the significance of Zion, see Marvin Tate, *Psalms 51-100*, Word Biblical Commentary 20 (Dallas: Word Books, 1990), p. 140; and H. J. Kraus, *Theology of the Psalms*, trans. Keith Crim (Minneapolis: Augsburg, 1986), pp. 93-106, esp. pp. 78-84.

15. For a more detailed treatment of the structure of Psalm 73 and the relative significance of verse 17 in comparison to verse 15, see J. Clinton McCann, Jr., "Psalm 73: A Microcosm of Old Testament Theology" in *The Listening Heart: Essays in Wisdom and the Psalms in Honor of Roland E. Murphy, O. Carm.*, eds. K. G. Hoglund et al. (JSOTSS 58; Sheffield, England: JSOT Press, 1987), pp. 249-50.

16. Walter Brueggemann, "Bounded by Obedience and Praise: The Psalms as Canon," *JSOT* 50 (1991):86.

17. The observation that Book III is communally oriented and reflects the experience of exile is not new; see, for instance, A. F. Kirkpatrick, *The Book of Psalms* (Cambridge, England: Cambridge University Press, 1921), pp. 427-30.

18. Brueggemann, "Bounded by Obedience and Praise," p. 81.

19. Quoted in Maurice Friedman, *Martin Buber's Life and Work: The Later Years, 1945-1965* (New York: E. P. Dutton, Inc., 1983), p. 418; see pp. 314, 410-12. See also Buber's essay "The Heart Determines: Psalm 73" in *Theodicy in the Old Testament*, ed. J. L. Crenshaw (Philadelphia: Fortress Press, 1983), pp. 109-18.

20. See, however, Mitchell Dahood, *Psalms II, 51-100*, Anchor Bible 17 (Garden City, N.Y.: Doubleday, 1968), p. 195, who, like many scholars, sees an allusion to the assumptions of Enoch and Elijah (Gen. 5:24; 2 Kings 2:11), but who also argues that "the psalmist finds the solution to the inconsistencies of this life in the final reward of the righteous after death."

9. GOD'S SPACE AND GOD'S TIME

1. See above on Psalm 46:4-7 and note 15 of chapter 8. Some of the following material on Psalms 48 and 122 also appears in my essay "Preaching on Psalms for Advent," *Journal for Preachers* [P. O. Box 520; Decatur, GA. 30031-0520] 16 (Advent 1992): 11-16.
2. Robert Alter, *The Art of Biblical Poetry* (New York: Basic Books, 1985), p. 124; I am indebted to several of Alter's insights found on pp. 121-29.
3. Ibid., p. 122; italics added.
4. Ibid., p. 133.
5. Elie Wiesel, *A Beggar in Jerusalem* (New York: Pocket Books, 1970), p. 19.
6. Ibid., p. 20.
7. See also Mark 13:1-2, 14:58, 15:29, where the Gospel writer suggests that Jesus has replaced the Temple; that is, Jesus is the new locus of God's revelation in space and time. The Gospel of Luke makes the same affirmation by having the disciples meet the risen Christ in *Jerusalem*, not in Galilee as in Matthew and Mark. As in Psalm 48, the particularity of Jerusalem and Jesus is but the starting point for a message that is to extend "to all nations" (Luke 24:47); see N. Perrin, *The Resurrection According to Matthew, Mark, and Luke* (Philadelphia: Fortress Press, 1977), pp. 66-71.
8. Walker Percy, *The Second Coming* (New York: Ivy Books, 1980), p. 307.
9. Ibid., p. 328.
10. See Gerald H. Wilson, "The Use of Royal Psalms at the 'Seams' of the Hebrew Psalter," *JSOT* 35 (1986): 92, and *The Editing of the Hebrew Psalter*, SBL Dissertation Series 76 (Chico, Calif.: Scholars Press, 1985), p. 215; see above, chap. 2.
11. The translation is that of Patrick D. Miller, Jr., *Interpreting the Psalms* (Philadelphia: Fortress Press, 1986), p. 126. The Hebrew verbs are *yld*, the most frequent Hebrew verb for bearing children, and *ḥûl* (see Isa. 51:2; Job 39:1; Ps. 29:9).
12. See Alter, *The Art of Biblical Poetry*, p. 127.
13. Ibid., p. 127.
14. Miller, *Interpreting the Psalms*, p. 127.
15. See Douglas John Hall, *God and Human Suffering: An Exercise in the Theology of the Cross* (Minneapolis: Augsburg, 1986), pp. 49-62.
16. Reinhold Niebuhr, *The Irony of American History* (New York: Charles Scribner's Sons, 1952), p. 63.

CONCLUSION: THE PSALMS AND JESUS CHRIST

1. See Patrick D. Miller, Jr., *Interpreting the Psalms* (Philadelphia: Fortress Press, 1986), pp. 27-28.
2. H. J. Kraus, *Theology of the Psalms*, trans. Keith Crim (Minneapolis: Augsburg, 1986), p. 194. Kraus's final chapter is a comprehensive treatment of the use of the Psalms in the New Testament; see pp. 177-203.
3. See Walter Brueggemann, *Message of the Psalms* (Minneapolis: Augsburg Press, 1984), p. 143.
4. See Kraus, *Theology of the Psalms*, p. 196; see chapter 4 above.
5. See ibid., p. 193.
6. I am indebted to the insights of James L. Mays, "Psalm 118 in the Light of Canonical Analysis" in *Canon, Theology, and Old Testament Interpretation: Essays in Honor of Brevard Childs*, eds. Gene M. Tucker, David L. Peterson, Robert R. Wilson (Philadelphia: Fortress Press, 1988), pp. 299-311.

7. See James L. Mays, "Prayer and Christology: Psalm 22 as Perspective on the Passion," *Theology Today* 42 (October 1985):322.

8. For a helpful summary of the quotations and allusions in the Passion story to Psalm 22 and other psalms and Old Testament texts, see John H. Reumann, "Psalm 22 at the Cross: Lament and Thanksgiving for Jesus Christ," *Interpretation* 28 (1974):40-42.

9. Mays, "Prayer and Christology," p. 324.

10. Ellen F. Davis, "Exploding the Limits: Form and Function in Psalm 22," *JSOT* 53 (1992):100; see pp. 97, 103.

11. Ibid., p. 103; italics added.

12. Mays, "Prayer and Christology," p. 324.

13. Davis, "Exploding the Limits," p. 97.

14. See Miller, *Interpreting the Psalms,* pp. 106-7.

15. Davis, "Exploding the Limits," pp. 102-3.

16. Ibid., pp. 103-5.

17. Mays, "Prayer and Christology," p. 329.

18. Ibid., p. 330.

APPENDIX: THE SINGING OF THE PSALMS

1. See John H. Eaton, *The Psalms Come Alive* (London: Mowbray, 1984).

2. See Suzanne Haik-Vantoura, *The Music of the Bible—Revealed* (San Francisco: Bibal Press/K.D.H., Inc., 1990).

3. *The Book of Order* (Louisville: Office of the General Assembly, Presbyterian Church [U.S.A.], 1992), section W-2. 1003.

4. Used by permission of Hal H. Hopson; see *Reformed Liturgy and Music* 23/1 (Winter 1989):30.

5. This entire issue of *Reformed Liturgy and Music* is devoted to the Psalter, as are Volumes 23/1 (Winter 1989) and 14/4 (Fall 1980). These three volumes provide an excellent introduction to the history and use of the Psalms in worship.

SCRIPTURE INDEX

OLD TESTAMENT

NEW TESTAMENT

Acts, *continued*
9:13	107
9:26	107
9:29	107

Romans
1–11	108
3:28	26
3:31	26
4:6-8	111
5:8	120
8:16-17	91
8:39	87, 144
12:1-2	108
14:7-8	146

1 Corinthians
1:23	99
1:31	108
6:19-20	67
11:23-24	151
11:26	121
12:26	117
15:58	144

2 Corinthians
4:8	130
5:17	152
5:17-20	105
11:30	108
12:5-10	108

Galatians
2:16	26
2:20	105
6:2	117

Ephesians
| 4:11-16 | 37 |

Philippians
| 2:5-11 | 63 |

Colossians
| 1:15-20 | 63 |
| 3:16 | 163 |

1 Thessalonians
| 5:16-18 | 90 |

Hebrews
1:3-4	63
2:9	63
8:5	63

Revelation
5:9	171
14:3	171
15:3-4	171
21:22	138
22:1-2	138
22:2	138